GUNS OF REDEMPTION
AND THE
ROSCOE BATTLE

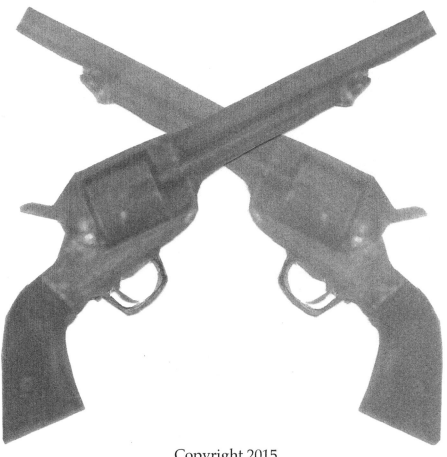

The Cover:©
Photo: The Author

Other graphics and photos:
US History Images
Public Domain
Library of Congress
Walt Ryan from his web page: www.SundowntrailBlog. com

Guns of Monegaw
AND THE
Roscoe Battle

Copyright © 2015
Meredith Isaac Anderson

For more information, please write:
Meredith Anderson
fisherman.anderson@juno.com

This book is a work of true history. Real locations and public figures are mentioned, but some characters described in this book may be fictionalized to enhance the reader's experience. The events described in this book are true as reported in newspapers, letters and archival government records of the period.

Manufactured in the United States of America.

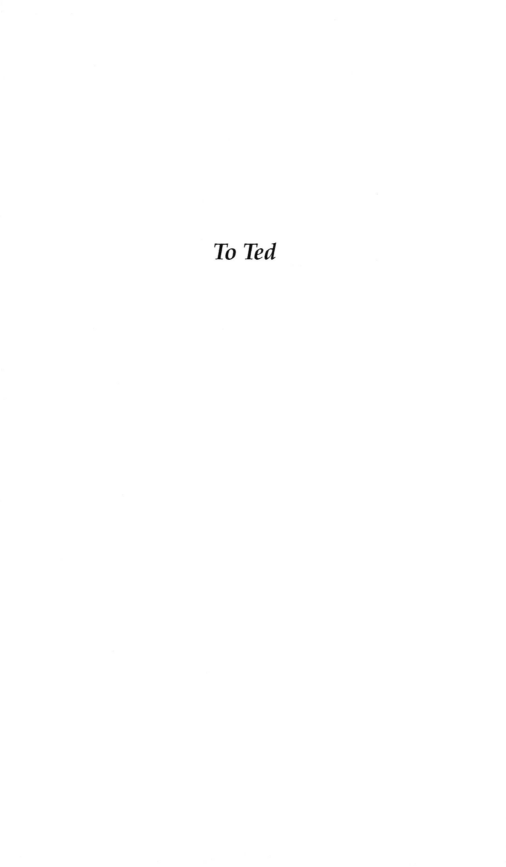

To Ted

Acknowledgements...

I would like to offer special thanks to those who encouraged me in this endeavor, especially Nikki Hansen, retired Professor and Head of the English Department from Weber State University in Ogden, Utah, my alma mater.

I would be remiss not to mention my wife, Linda, a historian and author in her own right, who became my best friend over forty-eight years ago when I was a young sailor in Uncle Sam's Seventh Fleet.

My brother, Levor Oldham, the true and loyal friend who is always there.

And a SPECIAL THANKS to the fine people of Missouri who have made me feel at home and gave my assistance with my research for this piece.

Table Of Contents

Chapter 1

Pinkertons

On August 25, 1819, Allan Pinkerton was born in Glasgow, Scotland.

As a young man he loved to work with his hands and was always interested in solving puzzles of how things worked and the mechanics of tools. He soon found himself working as a barrel maker, but unemployment and the slipping economy of his native Scotland caused him to seek other avenues for his skills.

At the age of 23 he took his savings and immigrated to the United States where he found a demand for his skills. He became a barrel maker in Chicago.

A stout young man of strong stature, he liked to join his fellow barrel makers at a nearby pub after working hours where he met other young men from the community and shared after work drinks. He was often involved in breaking up fights and settling disputes in a peaceful manner.

It was after one such altercation that he met and became friends with a young man who was a member of the Chicago police force. His new friend, Edward, was a policeman and the two men often discussed cases that the young officer was working on.

It became apparent the young Scot had an uncanny knack for treating the mysteries of a case like a puzzle and was able to discern the cause of the crime being investigated and point the young officer in the direction of a solution.

One evening when Edward came into the pub, he was accompanied by an older man in a suit. They joined Allan at a table and began to discuss a new case that was a real puzzle. The wife of a local merchant had been murdered for no apparent reason.

Allan convinced them that discovering the motivation for the murder would lead to the killer. It was Allan's thought that most murders were committed because of greed, personal gain or revenge and although there was no robbery involved in this case, there had to be a motive of personal gain for someone.

Within a week Edward was back to tell explain to Allan that the apparently grief stricken merchant turned out to be the killer. It turned out that the merchant had a mistress on the side and she had given him an ultimatum or she would leave him.

In 1847 Pinkerton joined the Chicago police force and in 1849 he was appointed to the position of Detective. His only duty was to solve the crimes of the city.

In 1850, Allan Pinkerton joined his brother Robert, who had been working as an investigator for railroads and other industrially related businesses, founding the Pinkerton National Detective Agency, locating their office at 80 Washington Street in Chicago.

Pinkerton immediately set up his Pinkerton Code:
Accept no bribes.
Never compromise with criminals.
Partner with local law enforcement agencies.
Refuse divorce cases or cases that initiate scandals.
Turn down reward money.
Never raise fees without the client's knowledge.
Keep clients apprised on an on-going basis.

Sign adopted by Allan and Robert Pinkerton

By 1853 the reputation of the Pinkerton detective agency was particularly good and they were being called upon to work with law enforcement to solve cases all over the United States.

By 1855 the detective agency's notoriety and popularity had grown so much the agency was being recruited by express companies all over the mid-western states (at that time those states were the western frontier) to protect money that they were shipping by railroad.

In 1856, Allan Pinkerton hired Kate Warne to become the first female detective in the United States. It is not long before she is his lead female detective and because of the company's sound reputation for the highest integrity, he begins hiring other female detectives, saying: "In my service you will serve your country better than on the field. I have several female operatives. If you agree to come aboard you will go in training with the head of my female detectives, Kate Warne. She has never let me down."

Kate Warne as Union interrogator

3

There was unquestioned integrity on the part of every Pinkerton detective. They became famous for their honesty to the point that a citizen wishing to reenforce his honesty or integrity would say, "I Pinkerton swear." Perhaps that is where today's "pinky swear" comes from.

In 1861 Allan Pinkerton, hired by the new Republican political party, uncovered a plot to assassinate the newly elected Republican President, Abraham Lincoln. He was instrumental in moving Lincoln through the ranks of Democratic insurrectionists in Maryland to his first inauguration.

During the Civil War, Pinkerton acted as head of the Union Intelligence Service, the forerunner of the Secret Service and was instrumental in the protection of the president.

It is during this period that Allan Pinkerton began to keep records on individuals he came into contact with as a result of his job.

In 1861, with the onset of the Civil War, Major General George B. McClellan was given command of the Army of the Potomac defending Washington.

General McClellan

Allan Pinkerton was assigned as chief of intelligence. Often using the alias Major Allen or E. J. Allen, his responsibilities included collecting intelligence on the enemy and for counterintelligence activities against enemy agents.

Allan Pinkerton

The majority of the intelligence Pinkerton collected was the result of careful questioning and debriefing of people who had come to the north across Confederate lines.

There was a wide variety of people to be interrogated: Confederate Army prisoners captured by Union forces, civilians escaping the fighting, businessmen with interests in both north and south.

He soon discovered that the best information about supply depots, camps and fortifications was coming in from escaped slaves. He issued orders to his investigators that they should put extra effort into the debriefing of former slaves. He instructed them to be on the lookout for former slaves who had some education or seemed particularly skilled in observation or remembering military details. If a person was recognized to have these qualities, he or she would be sent directly to Pinkerton for a personal interview.

From this small group of slaves, Pinkerton recruited members for his "black intelligence" group. The best known of these was Pinkerton agent John Scobell who was recruited in the fall of 1861.

The *Free* slave of a Scotsman from Mississippi, Scobell was well educated. His former master had told him to "Scat" when the war broke out in earnest with shooting on both sides.

The sturdy young black American was a great roll player and could think on his feet in the most stressful situations.

Teaming up with Pinkerton agents such as Timothy Webster and Mrs. Carrie Lawton, one of Pinkerton's best female operatives, he acted as a servant, cook, food vendor or laborer. While the white agents were often suspected of soliciting information and sometimes closely watched, no one paid any notice to the comings and goings of a household servant.

Scobell was a member in long-standing of a secret Negro organization called the "Legal League." He used this relationship with the black community to collect information on local conditions, moral, fortifications and troop disposition. He is credited with providing valuable intelligence on Confederate order of battle, supplies and troop movements. League members helped Scobell with the collection of information and many worked as couriers, passing the gathered intelligence through the Confederate lines.

Pinkerton told the story of the escape of agent Mrs. Lawton where Scobell was instrumental in protecting her from pursuing Confederate agents.

Pinkerton worked as General McClellan's Chief of Intelligence until 1862 when McClellan was sacked by President Lincoln for inaction and General Ambrose E. Bunside took over the Army of the Patomac.

Posted elsewhere for the remainder of the war, it was during this period that Pinkerton developed a liking for the double action Tranter revolver made in England. Because this pistol was double action, squeezing the trigger would rotate the cylinder to bring the next round into firing position and at the same time cock the hammer back.

Not only did Pinkerton prefer this weapon, but so did the majority of his detectives.

Tranter Revolver

Calibre: 44in (11.2mm)
Weight: .88kg (31oz)
Length: 292mm (11.5in)
Barrel length: 165mm (6.5in)
Effective range: 20m (61ft)
Feed: five-round cylinder
Muzzle velocity: 168mps (550fps)
Country of origin: United kingdom

Tranter revolver picture reprinted with permission from works by the author Walt Ryan from his web page: www.SundowntrailBlog. com. *Thanks Walt. M.I.A.*

This double action saved the shooter time, the smoother action of this motion made it much more accurate in a situation that required the shooter to fire more than one shot.

After the Civil War, Pinkerton returned to Chicago and continued in his detective agency.

On October 6, 1866, a moving train on the Ohio and Mississippi Railroad was stopped in a sparsely populated section of Jackson County, Indiana and robbed of $13,000.

There had been many burglaries and robberies of trains while at the station, but this daring day time robbery committed by the Reno brothers was a first in American history and of course, the express company called Pinkerton to investigate. None of the money was recovered.

In 1868 Robert Pinkerton died.

On the evening of October 7, 1871, Chicago caught fire and on the third day, when the Great Fire had burned itself out, the business district of the city had been destroyed. Among other things, the fire also claimed the headquarters of the Pinkerton Detective Agency and a majority of their records. Marshal Law was declared throughout the city and detectives from the Pinkerton Agency were hired to protect the city from looters.

Robert's widow, Alice Isabella Pinkerton, and his children were among those left homeless. When she turned to Allan for help, he offered to pay for the family's passage back to England. Alice accepted his offer and she and her sons sailed for Liverpool, England. The agency was now under the control of Allan and his sons.

Chapter 2

The James Boys

After their marriage, Robert Sallee James and his wife Zerelda (Cole) James, migrated to Missouri from Kentucky and settled in Clay County near what is now Kearny, Missouri, north of Kansas City. Robert acquired 100 acres of land and with the help of his slaves, he began to raise hemp and tobacco for commercial sale.

Robert was well educated and an ordained minister of the Baptist faith. He helped found William Jewell College in Liberty, Missouri.

On January 10, 1843, the James' had the first of three children, Alexander Franklin "Frank" James. Four years later on September 5, 1847, Jesse Woodson James was born. Two years later, their daughter, Susan Lavenia was born on November 25, 1849.

Sad times came to the James farm when suddenly in 1851, Robert became ill and died unexpectedly. A few months later, Zerelda married Benjamin Simms in 1852. But alas, two years later, he too passed away.

When Frank was twelve and Jesse eight, their mother married for the third time. This time to Doctor Reuben Samuel in 1855.

All of the James children attended school regularly and Frank took a particular interest in a collection of books that his father had by William Shakespeare. Frank, a child of studious nature, professed early on that he would be a teacher some day.

9

During 1854, Congress, under the leadership of Democrat, Henry Clay, with the help of Stephen A. Douglas, Democrat from Illinois, pushed the Kansas-Nebraska Act through Congress. The law, designed to put an end to the "Underground Railroad" and make it possible for each territory that applied for statehood to decide for themselves - by popular vote - whether they would be a "Slave" or "Free Labor" state, a state where slavery would be illegal. By 1855 this new law was causing much distress among the citizens of Clay County. Several families had migrated to Kansas in an effort to influence the slavery question and the vote.

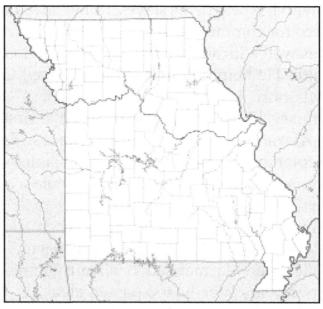

Missouri, August 10, 1820

Soon, militia units grew up on both sides of the border and persecuted people on the opposite side for their views of the political question. But, the primary goal of these bands of roving predators was to plunder and steal whatever they could from the other side.

After a northern militia from Lawrence, Kansas raided Liberty, Missouri and took two wagon loads of tanned red leather, the men of that militia cut up the leather, making leggings. Thus, the dreaded "Red Legs" came into being.

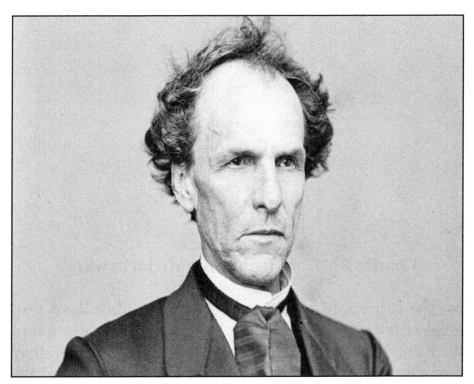

James Henry Lane "Mr. Red Leg"

And so went the "bleeding" of Kansas. In April, John Brown's verbal attacks on the pro-slavery legislature led a pro-slavery judge to issue warrants for the arrest of Brown and his sons.

On May 21, 1856 a band of over 750 pro-slavery men from Missouri rode into Lawrence, Kansas, waving banners proclaiming the supremacy of the white race. They ransacked the offices of two anti-slavery newspapers destroying the presses. They burned and looted homes and businesses along the main thoroughfare. During this raid only one person died - one of the raiders.

To defend against attacks of depredation, theft, and harassment on Free-State settlers, men such as James Henry Lane organized the "Red Legs," James Montgomery, and Charles R. Jennison organized "jayhawker units" that attacked pro-slavery families and communities.

Charles R. "Doc" Jennison, "Mr. Jayhawker"

The officers of these 'Red Leg' units may have professed the cause of advancing the anti-slavery position of their northern leadership, but for the common men, they seemed to be in it for the pilferage they could get and the cruelty they could deal out.

Another young man from Kansas that took advantage of the chaos during the "Bleeding Kansas" period was William Clarke Quantrill. Immigrating to Kansas in 1858, he began his robbing and stealing career by kidnapping slaves from Missouri farmers and selling them back.

When he was arrested for horse stealing, tried and scheduled to hang in Kansas, his gang took him out of jail and he fled to Missouri.

He continued his robbing, stealing and pillaging on both sides of the border until war broke out, when he began to concentrate on attacking Unionists.

William Clarke Quantrill
(July 31, 1837 – June 6, 1865)

In the U.S. Congress, January 29th, 1861, Kansas was admitted into the Union as a Free Labor State. The question that had caused the 'bleeding of Kansas' was answered. There was no longer a cause for the pro and anti-slavery factions to be fighting. Kansas was a "free" state.

'Red Leg' leader, Jim Lane was elected to the U.S. Senate to represent Kansas and Charles Robinson was elected the first governor of the new state of Kansas.

The fighting seemed to be over, but the indiscriminate stealing of livestock was not. William Quantrill and his band were still very much in business.

The admission of Kansas as a "free state" meant there were two more anti-slavery votes in Congress and the abolition of slavery could not be far behind.

For the south, the writing was on the wall. Because of the high population base in the north and the influx of European emigrants, the House of Representatives, had for several years been dominated by an anti-slavery sentiment. Kansas, being admitted as a "free labor" state meant that there were now more anti-slavery votes in the US Senate than ever before. Southern leaders now saw that if Lincoln was elected, the entire government voting block would be anti-slavery.

South Carolina - and other southern states - announced publicly that if the "abolitionist Republican," Abraham Lincoln were elected, they would secede from the Union.

Abraham Lincoln - 16th President

South Carolina was the first state to secede from the Union. On April 12, 1861 Confederate forces under the command of General P.G.T. Beauregard began a cannon barrage on the Union garrison at Fort Sumter in Charleston Harbor. Union Major Robert Anderson surrendered the fort at 2:30 p.m. on April 13 and was evacuated on the 14th. The United States and the newly formed Confederate States of America were at war.

On April 15 President Lincoln called on all the states that had not submitted 'notice of secession' to send fifteen thousand troops each to aid in the defense of Washington and the suppression of the Southern uprising.

Governor Claiborne Jackson of Missouri gave a speech and announced publicly that Missouri would not send a single man to "subjugate her sister states to the south."

The war had begun and Missouri plantation owner, Mark Gill, did not want "those damn Yankees" to get their hands on his slaves, so he rounded them up to take them to Texas. He hired Quantrill and his bunch to help make the move which involved a large wagon train.

In Quantrill's ranks rode an eighteen year old recruit from Clay County, the stepson on a slave owner, Frank James.

Frank James met and became friends with a man from Jackson County, Thomas Coleman "Cole" Younger. They, along with William Quantrill, later engaged the Union Army at the "Battle of Wilson's Creek," which was a Confederate victory.

"Bloody Bill" William T. Anderson
(1840 – October 26, 1864)

15

Not to be outdone, Frank's little brother, Jesse James fellin with a fellow Kentuckian, William T. Anderson - who would later earn the title of "Bloody Bill." At the battle of Centralia, sixteen year old Jesse James fired the volley that ended the life of Union Mounted Infantry Major Johnston.

16 Year old Bushwhacker Jesse W. James
(September 5, 1847 – April 3, 1882)

Dr. Reuben Samuel and Zerelda James, Jesse's mother, had four children together: Sarah Louisa, John Thomas, Fannie Quantrell, and Archie Peyton Samuel. To show the James' allegiance to the Bushwhacker leaders, little Fannie's middle name coming from the name of the Bushwhacker leader, William Clarke Quantrill and Jesse's half brother Archie Samuel received his name from Little Archie Clement, second in command of Bloody Bill Anderson's Bushwhackers.

Chapter 3

The Younger Boys

Henry Washington Younger and his wife Bersheba Leighton Fristoe Younger settled on a farm in Jackson County, Missouri, south of present day Kansas City. The family moved to Harrisonville, still further south in Cass County in 1857. In 1859 Henry was assigned the job of second mayor of that city.

Henry and Bersheba had fourteen children, ten girls and four boys. Thomas Coleman "Cole," was the eldest boy, born in 1844. James Hardin "Jim," was born in '48, John Harrison was born in '51 and Robert Ewing "Bob," was born in '53.

Henry was a very successful farmer and businessman. He often traveled between his home and town carrying large sums of money and was robbed several times.

On July 20, 1862 Henry was traveling to Kansas City on business, carrying $1,500. About one mile south of Westport he was accosted by a gang of Union "Jayhawkers" from Kansas. Not caring that he was a known Union sympathizer, he was shot three times in the back and killed. At first, it was thought that his death was a robbery gone bad. But, it was soon discovered that his murder was politically motivated; after all, he was a Missouri man and there was a war going on. Kansas Red Legs roamed freely across the land, robbing and killing both Union and Confederate sympathizers.

17

Just south of Osceola, at the confluence of the Osage and the Sac (Sauk) Rivers, Major General "Old Pap" Price, former governor of Missouri, had set up a recruiting base. It was through this base that eighteen year old Cole Younger joined the Confederate cause.

In July, prior to the Red Leg attack on Osceola, "Old Pap" had led his new recruits to the south with then governor Clayborn Jackson, who was fleeing before Union troops led by General Lyon.

Lyon caught up to the Confederate army near Springfield, Missouri and the Battle of Wilson Creek began. Unfortunately for General Lyon, General Price had been reenforced by General McColloch.

A young man wearing a red wool shirt distinguished himself, leading several cavalry charges against the Northern flank. His name was William Clarke Quantrill.

The battle, often called the "Bull Run" of the west, was an important victory for the Confederate Army.
Shortly after this battle, Cole joined Quantrill's raiders and became an important member of that company as well a close friend of Frank James.

On September 23, 1861, Kansas Red Legs under the command of General James Lane rode into Osceola, Missouri, the third largest city in the state at the time and burned it to the ground after plundering and pillaging the residents.

The sleepy little city was awakened to Union cannons, located in the town's cemetery, shelling the court house in the center of town.

The primary goal of the attacking force was to gain as much booty as they could. The Chaplain of the Union troops stole the pulpit and pews out of an Osceola church to take back to a new church he was building in Lawrence, Kansas.

Known for the quality and quantity of liquor, Osceola

produced and exported made this raid a favorite with the members of the Red Leg band. General Lane gave orders that the liquor that could not be carried off in wagons was to be burned or poured into the Osage River. He left the city with two hundred men carried in wagons as they were too drunk to sit a horse.

Twelve residents were shot on the square when they refused to turn over the forty thousand dollars in gold that had been in the bank's safe. With a detachment of six hundred men and a battery of cannons, Lane was unable to obtain the gold he came for.

The Red Legs burned town after town, some more than once. Robbing and killing was a way of life for the 'Jay-hawkers.'

On August 21, 1863, Quantrill and several other Bushwhacker leaders decided that they had had enough.

Cole Younger participated in the notorious raid against Lawrence, Kansas where some 200 men and boys were killed and the town was ransacked and burned. However, of the men killed, 70 were Union troops garrisoned on the outskirts of Lawrence. In 1864 Cole's brother, James, joined Quantrill's band.

Cole went south to take a commission in the Confederate Cavalry as a captain. He led a company of men into Louisiana and later to California, where he remained until the close of the war.

Cole returned to his home in 1865. In the meantime, James had been captured by Union troops in the same ambush that resulted in William Quantrill's death. He was then sent to Alton prison.

Cole and James came home to the family farm to find it in ruins and the once profitable business was long gone. Though brothers, John and Bob, had worked hard to keep the farm up, the ravages of war had left it in ruins.

Chapter 4

The Aftermath of War

The government of the state of Missouri had begun a program of emancipating the slaves in the state on a gradual basis in 1863.

By the time the war ended, the Republicans in the state demanded the immediate and unconditional emancipation of all slaves.

In 1865, the General Assembly voted for a convention to be held to consider changes to the Missouri Constitution of 1820. The convention lasted from January 6 until April 10, 1865. The delegates wrote a completely new Constitution because much of the 1820 constitution had been written by pro-slavery southerners.

Charles D. Drake, a vocal, uncompromising and Radical Republican who by vocation was an experienced lawyer, led the Constitutional Convention.

Charles D. Drake
The inexperienced delegates to the convention allowed

Drake to lead the way and relied on him for the formulation of the new Constitution, which became known as the Drake Constitution. There was such a distrust of the slave owners of the state that Drake wielded great power during the convention. His only true opposition came from the German community because of Drake's anti-immigrant stance.

The new Constitution banned the practice of slavery without exception. In addition, it restricted the rights of former rebels and rebel sympathizers.

Article 2 introduced the part of the constitution that became known as the "Ironclad" or "Cocklebur" Oath. It required teachers, lawyers, clergy, and anyone else who wanted to vote to promise that they had not committed a long list of disloyal acts during the war. This group of professionals was targeted as individuals because of their influence over the youth and general population.

With support from rural delegates, mostly small farmers new to the state, Drake forced the removal of all officers of the community. Judges, prosecuting attorneys and sheriffs were thrown out of office. The right to vote was given only to those who had been loyal to the Union during the war. This ensured the election of Radical Republicans to all the newly vacated positions.

The vote to ban slavery in the Constitution was approved almost unanimously. Only four members of the convention voted against it.
William S. Holland of Henry County introduced a resolution that would become part of Article 4, which forbade the General Assembly from compensating slave owners for the loss of their "property."

Another major part of the new Constitution, the "Ironclad Oath," was so severe that many Unionist men refused to take it. It was said that the oath was equivalent to "trying to ride a horse with a cocklebur under your saddle." The German community who had fiercely defended the Union during the war, opposed the draconian limitations imposed on individuals by the oath. However, the Radicals, many of whom suffered cruelties at the hands of pro-South guerillas, made sure the oath became a part of the Constitution.

The Constitution did more than emancipate slaves and restrict voting rights. In many ways it was very progressive. It created free public schools, although they were segregated. It also forbade the government to lend its credit to private individuals or corporations. The Constitution, for all of its benefits, failed to provide true equality for the African American population it freed. They would not receive the right to vote until the passage of the 17th Amendment to the U.S. Constitution in 1870, five years later.

The Drake Constitution, officially known as the Missouri Constitution of 1865, was adopted by the state legislature on April 8, 1865. It was then sent to the people for ratification.

The ratification of the Drake Constitution by the state's population came down to just a few votes. The eastern part of the state and central parts of Missouri rejected it. But great support from the northwestern and southwestern regions where guerillas had terrorized loyal citizens and that portion of the population that had been Union soldiers on the battlefield gave the Constitution a narrow victory.

This constitution that gave the returning Confederate Veteran virtually no rights created a great deal of anger and frustration.

Farms with back taxes that had accrued during the war years and banks unwilling to make loans to former Confederates resulted in veterans having to sell large portions of their property to keep any. Many Confederates "pulled up stakes" and moved west to Texas or Cali-fornia.

An embittered Cole Younger was no different and continued to associate with his old war comrades. In the midst of the tumultuous Reconstruction in Missouri, some former soldiers became outlaws.

After the death of "Bloody Bill" Anderson in an ambush by Union militia on October 27, 1864, Little Archie Clement took command, continuing to fight into the next year.

Following the surrender of General Robert E. Lee's army in Virginia, Clement continued to fight, even demanding the surrender of the Missouri town of Lexington.

Though some of his fellow Bushwhackers, including Dave Pool, surrendered, Clement and Jesse James remained under arms.

On May 15, 1865, Clement and James attempted to surrender to a Union cavalry patrol that they encountered near Lexington, Missouri. A skirmish ensued in which James was severely wounded, suffering the second of two life-threatening chest wounds.

Jesse recovered from his chest wound at his uncle's boardinghouse in Harlem, Missouri (north across the Missouri River from the City of Kansas' River Quay [changed to Kansas City in 1889]), where he was tended to by his first cousin, Zerelda "Zee" Mimms, named after Jesse's mother.   Jesse and his cousin began a nine-year courtship, culminating in marriage.

While Jesse was recovering, his old pal, Archie Clement kept his bushwhacker gang together and began to harass Republican authorities.

In 1866, Clement's gang took up a new profession: bank robbery, especially banks associated with Missouri Unionists and railroads.

On February 13, 1866, a group of gunmen carried out the first daylight, peacetime, armed bank robbery in U.S. history.

They held up the Clay County Savings Association in Liberty, Missouri, reportedly stealing more than $58,000 in cash and bonds. The bank was owned and operated by former Union militia officers, who had recently conducted the first Republican Party rally in Clay County's history.

Some historians believe the actual amount of cash and bonds taken ranged between $20,000 and $38,000. The bank's loss was inflated to make the incident more notorious.

State authorities suspected Archie Clement of leading the raid, accompanied by Jesse James, and offered a reward for Archie's capture. In later years, the list of suspects would grow to include Frank James, Cole Younger, John Jarrette, Oliver Shepard, Bud and Donny Pence, Frank Gregg, Bill and James Wilkerson, Joab Perry, Ben Cooper, Red Mankus and Allen Parmer (who later married Susan James, Frank and Jesse's sister).

During the escape through the streets of Liberty, one of the gang shot and killed an innocent bystander named George Wymore. It was this killing attributed to Jesse that got him branded as a cold blooded killer and thrust him into national notoriety. A string of robberies followed, many linked to the Clement's gang.

Little Archie was identified during the hold-up of the Alexander Mitchell and Company in Lexington, Missouri, on October 30, 1866, in which the gang stole $2,000. (This figure was not inflated.)

On election day in 1866 Little Archie led a hundred former Bushwhackers into Lexington, Missouri. Disrupting the voting process, they influenced the election so that the Republican party lost control of the government. Governor Thomas C. Fletcher immediately sent a platoon of state militia, led by Major Bacon Montgomery after Clement.

On December 13, 1866 "Little Archie" was having a few

drinks with a friend in Lexington. Major Montgomery sent a squad of men to apprehend Clement, who was wanted on a warrant for the Liberty, Missouri robbery.

The major's men called out for Clement to surrender. Clement drew his revolvers and a wild gun battle followed. Despite having sustained a gunshot wound to the chest, Archie managed to make it outside and onto his horse. He rode up the town's main street in an effort to escape only to be shot from his horse by a militiaman stationed at the courthouse.

Major Montgomery and his men approached the fallen bushwhacker, who, though mortally wounded, was trying to cock his revolver with his teeth.

One of the soldiers asked, "Arch, you are dying. What do you want me to do with you?" Clement replied, "I've done what I always said I would do ... die before I'd surrender." Major Montgomery himself later stated of Clement's final moments, "I've never met better 'grit' on the face of the earth."

After Archie Clement's death, his gang continued to rob and be pursued by all branches of law enforcement, including federal troops.

In 1868 Frank and Jesse James allegedly joined Cole Younger in robbing a bank at Russellville, Kentucky.

Jesse James did not become famous until December 7, 1869, when he and (most likely) Frank robbed the Daviess County Savings Association in Gallatin, Missouri. The robbery netted little money, but it appears that Jesse shot and killed the cashier, Captain John Sheets, mistakenly believing him to be Samuel P. Cox, the militia officer who had killed "Bloody Bill" Anderson during the Civil War.

Little Archie Clement

The James - Younger gang. Circa 1876. Back row: Bob
Younger, Jim Younger and Cole Younger.
Front Row: Clell Miller, Frank James and Jesse James.

Cox had earlier been a partner of the firm Ballinger, Cox & Kemper with Gallatin businessman J.M. Kemper whose son William Thornton Kemper, Sr. went on to found two of the largest banks headquartered in Missouri (Commerce Bancshares and UMB Financial Corporation) but the business relationship had dissolved by the time of the robbery.

James announced to witnesses in the bank that he was killing Cox (it was really Captain John Sheets) as revenge for Cox killing "Bloody Bill Anderson."

From the bank, he and Frank made their escape right through the middle of a posse. This put his name in the newspapers for the first time. The murder of John W. Sheets was truly a dastardly deed.

This 1869 robbery marked the emergence of Jesse James as the most famous of the former guerrillas and the first time he was publicly labeled an "outlaw," as Missouri Governor Thomas T. Crittenden set a reward for his capture.

Right after this robbery James wrote letters and created an alliance between himself and John Newman Edwards, editor and founder of the Kansas City Times. Edwards, a former Confederate cavalryman, was campaigning to re-turn former secessionists to power in Missouri.

Six months after the Gallatin robbery, Edwards published the first of many letters written by Jesse James to the public, asserting his innocence. Over time, the letters gradually became more political in tone, denouncing the Republicans and voicing James' pride in his Confederate loyalties. Together with Edwards's admiring editorials, the letters turned James into a symbol of Confederate defiance of Reconstruction.

Editorials written by Edwards praised Jesse James and ridiculed the wealthy railroads and banks that he robbed. This newspaper was virtually turning a robber and bandit into a folk hero.

The Adams Express Company hired the Pinkerton National Detective Agency in 1874 to stop the James-Younger gang. The Pinkerton agency worked primarily against urban professional criminals, as well as providing industrial security, such as strike breaking.

The James - Younger gang had friends throughout Missouri and received support from many former Confederates. As a result, they eluded the Pinkertons detectives.

Allan Pinkerton selected a special agent, Joseph Whicher, and dispatched him to infiltrate Zerelda Samuel's (Jesse James' mother) farm. It wasn't long before a report reached Pinkerton headquarters that their agent, Joseph Whicher had been found dead.

Infuriated by the news, Allan Pinkerton, took over the case as a personal vendetta. He began to work with former Unionists who lived near the James family farm. On the night of January 25, 1875, he staged a raid on the family farm. Detectives threw an incendiary device into the house; it exploded, killing James's young half-brother Archie (named for Archie Clement) and blowing off one of the arms of the James family's matriarch, Zerelda Samuel.

Afterward, Pinkerton denied that the raid's intent was arson, but biographer Ted Yeatman located a letter by Pinkerton in the Library of Congress in which Pinkerton declared his intention to "burn the house down."

The raid on the family home outraged the public and did more than all of Edwards's columns to create sympathy for Jesse James. The Missouri state legislature narrowly defeated a bill that praised the James and Younger brothers and offered them amnesty.

Every city and town had a dance hall or theater and the subject matter being presented by the actors on stage ranged from a monologue to a full blown play about how the James's were being put upon and persecuted by the nasty banks, railroads and their henchmen, the Pinkertons. The frustrated Pinkerton agency was becoming a laughing stock throughout the country.

Chapter 5

Gad's Hill Robbery

On January 31, 1874, the Iron Mountain Railroad was robbed at Gad's Hill in Wayne Country, Missouri. At 3:00 in the afternoon, five members of the James-Younger gang boarded the train and proceeded to rob the passengers.

While the exact amount has never been certain, newspapers at the time estimated between $2,000 and $22,000 was stolen. It is known that the leader of the band gave the railroad men a prepared press release. Thus, the suspicion that it was the James-Younger gang was intensified.

The express company called upon the Pinkerton Detective Agency to pursue the culprits. They were certain that the detectives were collecting their retainer fee and doing nothing.

An experienced Pinkerton detective was sent to Jackson County pretending to be a farmhand seeking employment - his goal to infiltrate the James farm near Kearny. He was gunned down on a Jackson County road by parties unknown. Allen Pinkerton blamed Frank and Jesse James, and the Pinkerton Agency was desperate to capture of kill any members of the James-Younger gang they could.

Robert and William Pinkerton were immediately dispatched with a large posse to locate and arrest the Youngers. After two weeks in the field, they were unable to develop any information leading to the arrest of the robbers.

Returning to their Chicago office, it was decided that a special train and posse would be sent to southwestern Missouri, to search out and capture any of the gang they could find.

They obtained information that led them to believe that two of the Youngers had gone into Arkansas and the whereabouts of the James boys were totally unknown, but it was reported that two of the Youngers had been seen in Saint Clair County.

The stages of the theaters in Chicago as well as those across the country were filled with stories of the daring young bandits and the inept detectives that pursued them. Allan Pinkerton declared that Jesse James was the worst man to ever cross the face of the earth and he needed to be done away with no matter what the cost. The Pinkerton office called in two of their best detectives to continue the pursuit of the train robbers.

Captain Louis L. Lull, a bright and genuine young man who had served as a Union officer during the Civil War and as a captain of detectives for the city of Chicago, was to lead the search. His second in command was James Wright, a former Confederate soldier who had served with men from Saint Clair County, Missouri.

Lull, a sturdy man of 27 years and Wright who was highly thought of as a successful agent.

The two men sortied into Missouri with a posse searching for any sign of the Youngers. They ventured into Monegaw Springs, an area known to be frequented by the Youngers when they were on the scout, (hiding out from the law.)

After spending a couple days in Monegaw Springs, Captain Lull sent his posse home. He was unaware that he had actually been in Monegaw Springs at the same time John Younger was there. John had been seen by them, but they didn't know his identity at the time.

The posse returned to Chicago but Captain Lull and James Wright remained in the field. They rode to Osceola where they registered at the Commercial Hotel. Lull checked in under the name of W. J. Allen to hide his true identity. He was concerned that someone might recognize his name as a Pinkerton detective.

The two agents passed themselves off as cattle buyers and, under this guise, were free to move about the town and hold discussions with the residents without raising undue interest.

Many of Osceola's residents were elderly. Their days were spent sitting around the city square whittling, chewing tobacco and spitting, while passing time in casual conversations.

By listening to these conversations and asking the right questions, the detectives were able to conclude that the Youngers were in the Monegaw Springs area. Probably around the Snuffer place which was located in the southeastern corner of the Montgomery Negro settlement.

The settlement was called "Montgomery" because that was the name of the family that owned them as slaves before the Civil War.

A dirt road ran from the Theodrick Snuffer place west past the McFarrin cabin and on across the Roscoe-Chalk-level road at the forks to Monegaw Springs.

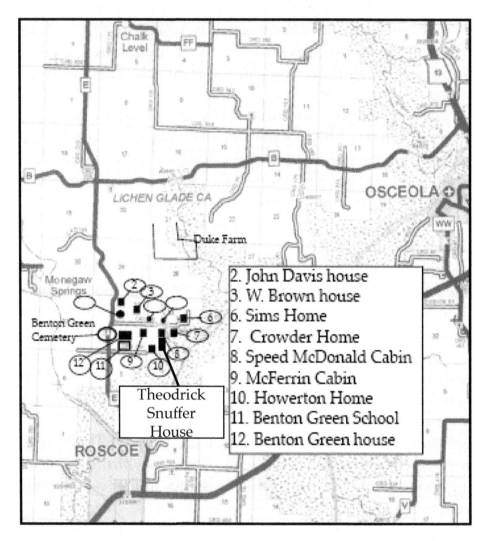

2. John Davis house
3. W. Brown house
6. Sims Home
7. Crowder Home
8. Speed McDonald Cabin
9. McFerrin Cabin
10. Howerton Home
11. Benton Green School
12. Benton Green house

Theodrick Snuffer House

Monegaw Springs area Map (Montgomery)

Chapter 6

The Towns

Osceola, in the year 1874, was a shadow of the bustling city it had been in 1861.

*****

Much of this chapter has been extracted and or copied from the great book by Richard F. Sunderwirth: Osceola, Missouri, The Burning of 1861. This exciting historically documented book is available at amazon.com. *Thank you Richard. M.I.A.*

Osceola, Missouri was, by no means, a sleepy little village in 1861. On the contrary, it was the third largest city in the state with a population in excess of 2000. It was a jewel of the South, located at the confluence of the Sac (Sauk) and Osage Rivers.

It was a bustling commercial center with warehouses full of goods such as coffee, flour, cornmeal, cotton and whiskey. Whiskey being a high value trade item, there were several distillers in the area.

Corn provided for the large volume of liquor being produced. It was abundant, but hard to transport. Reducing it to it smallest common denominator not only made it easier to transport but also made it more valuable than in its original state.

Two hundred slaves worked along the river front docks, loading and unloading riverboats that made the passage up the Osage River from the Missouri River.

General Sterling Price, a former governor of Missouri, set up a recruiting camp south of Osceola at the joining of the two rivers. A granite marker now sits on the bluff over- looking the confluence of the two rivers. It reads in part: *Here at the confluence of the Sauk (Sac) and Osage Rivers, from October through December, 1861, Major General Sterling Price of the Missouri State Guard maintained a recruitment camp. Of the 12,000 men gathered here 8,000 went with Price in the the Confederate States Army. 2,000 went home to protect their families, many to fight in bitter Guerrilla Warfare.*

While Missourians were busy defending their state, the destruction of Osceola had already been put in motion a thousand miles away in Washington, D.C. In a letter dated June 20, 1861, Abraham Lincoln wrote to his Secretary of War Cameron:

"My dear Sir: Since you spoke to me yesterday about General J.H. Lane, of Kansas, I have been reflecting upon the subject, and have concluded that we need the service of such a man out there at once; that we had better appoint him a brigadier-general of volunteers today, and send him off with such authority to raise a force (I think two regiments better than three, but as to this I am not particular) as you think will get him into actual work quickest. Tell him, when he starts, to put it through; not to be writing or telegraphing back here, but put it through" Yours truly,

A. Lincoln

This letter put into power one of the most dreadful figures in American history. He would soon earn the moniker "The Grim Chieftain." General Lane organized 1,200 troops and launched his attack on Missouri.

When General Price left Osceola to lead his army south to the August 10th *Battle of Wilson's Creek,* Lane, coming from the west, secretly crossed the Missouri border at Trading Post, Kansas and began his burning, murder, rape and plunder of Missourians.

General Price and General Ben McCulloch with poorly equipped and trained troops at this early stage of the war had a combined force nearly twice the size of Lyonl's. But the impetuous Union commander did not want to cede the region without a fight and attacked on August 10 at the battle of Oak Hill (Wilson's Creek).

General Price defeated the Union forces under General Sigel and General Nathaniel Lyon. Lyon was killed during this engagement.

Next he moved north to attack the Union stronghold of Lexington, Missouri. The battle lasted from September 13 to September 20, ending in Southern victory.

The attacks of 'border ruffians' (red legs) on the civilian population of Missouri was always for the plunder tat could be taken away after the rightful owner had been dispatched. The declaration of war in April of 1861 legitimized the action of such groups as the Kansas "Jayhawkers." They now killed and robbed in the name of the United States government.

Wanting vengeance and plunder for the pro-slavery attack on Lawrence, Kansas, five years earlier, General Lane moved with 600 'Red Legs' toward Osceola, a slumbering victim.

Lane said, "We believe in a war of extermination; there is no such thing as Union men in(side) the border of Missouri. I want to see every foot of ground in Jackson, Cass, and Bates counties in Missouri burned over, everything laid waste."

In a reference to marauding, he added, *"Everything disloyal from a shanghai rooster to a Durham cow must be leaned out."* Knowing what was in store for their town, a few men engaged the arriving army outside of town where some of their number were wounded or killed.

Approaching Osceola down cemetery ridge, Jim Lane's "Jayhawkers" set up cannons an opened fire on the courthouse, suspecting that there were pro-slavery men making a stand inside. Soon the night sky was bright as the courthouse burned.

To his credit, Lane ordered that "women and children should not be molested in any way."

While hundreds of shouting 'Jayhawkers' ran through the streets looting homes, shops, and barns, officers in an effort to prevent the men from getting drunk, tried to destroy large stocks of liquor (warehouses full) in the town.

Although 150 barrel heads were quickly smashed in, many Kansans nevertheless succeeded in filling their canteens and themselves. It has been recorded that n additional 300 barrels of whiskey were broken open and the contents dumped into the Osage River. Lane's men fell to the ground on the banks and lapped up as much liquor as they possibly could. Since a good deal of liquor had been consumed, many of the Union soldiers staggered through the streets of Osceola.

As the booze continued to flow toward the river, 'Red Legs' continued to stoop and fill as many of their canteens as they possible could for a littler personal enjoyment. Before long most of Lane's army was roaring drunk. The liquor soon became ignited like everything else in the town, and to the Osage River.

When no money was found in the bank, a drumhead courts-martial was held and twelve citizens were condemned to be shot.

From the business area the fire spread and leaped from house to house. It was not long before the entire city of magnificence and wealth was a smoking mass of ruins.

According to many writers, no one was allowed to remove anything from their burning houses. Most of the women and children could take nothing from their burning homes, not even the most personal and private items.

Alcohol was not the only spoil of war that the town of Osceola offered. Rev. Hugh Fisher, one of Lane's chaplains, made off with the altar furnishings from one of the local churches as well as all the church pews and the pulpit. This was to be used to complete his own church being built in Lawrence, Kansas. Lane, not to be outdone, selected a fine carriage, piano, and silk dresses for his wife, or perhaps some other female or females.

Negroes swarmed to Lane like flies around a carcass and were permitted to load themselves down with goods of every description. What was considered of little value or too bulky for easy removal was thrown into the streets or left in the homes or businesses to burn. When Lane left town, a long train of 200 wagons followed him filled with booty of all kinds. Among the masses of goods taken were boots, shoes, clothing, tons of pig lead, kegs of powder, percussion caps, supplies of cartridge paper, 3,000 sacks of flour, 50 sacks of coffee, slabs of bacon, barrels of brandy and whiskey, 500 pounds of sugar and molasses, assorted pieces of furniture, all types of camping equipment, and other pleasant knickknacks. Behind these wagons came 350 horses and 400 cattle, all stolen from Osceola citizens. Then came the long train of wagons filled with drunken soldiers. And behind them, near the end of Lane's ragtag procession, plodded a column of over 200 freed slaves.

This was a situation that became a fixture in the plundering processions of the Lane Brigade. At the very rear of the column came a mile-long stretch of "appropriated" wagons filled with slaves to young or old to walk as well as the black's belongings. The ex-slaves would be forced to travel in the dense dust cloud formed by the long train.

Lane had said earlier, "Slavery would not survive the march of the Union Army," and in this case, Lane was fulfilling his prophecy. It is written in various articles that well over a million dollars worth of goods actually left with him; however, it is safe to say Lane destroyed a great deal more than he carried away.

"As the sun went down Sunday night," concluded the brigade correspondent, *"Osceola was a heap of smoldering ruins. Well over two thousand people are left homeless and perhaps the fairest city in Missouri has been utterly wiped from the face of the earth."*

Lane's army left Osceola with all of their plunder and headed for Kansas, leaving old age and helpless innocents to keep vigil over the dead and wounded. Blood mixed with tears marked the spot where only a few short hours before had been peaceful, contented, happy homes.

*****

Many historians believe the population of the town at the time of the burning on September 21 & 22, 1861 could easily have been in the neighborhood of 3,000 people.

Osceola was now a sleepy little town on the banks of the Osage River with a population of 354 people.

The town still boasted one of the finest hotels in all of southwestern Missouri, the Commercial Hotel. It also had a a newspaper. This was the county seat and the office of the Saint Clair county sheriff.

The warehouses along its docks still served as the distribution point for no less than eleven counties in the area.

Roscoe

With a population of 312, Roscoe was a bustling little town on the banks of the Osage River, just nine miles from Osceola. It was the last stop for the steam boats coming up river.

Many of the people from the settlement of Montgomery worked at the docks in Roscoe. Other residents worked in the restaurants and at the Roscoe House. They also worked in Monegaw Springs.

Chalk Level (Township)

A township is 26 sections of unincorporated land that can be incorporated for the purpose of forming a town or city government within a county. The township of Chalk Level had a population of 864 folks dedicated primarily to farming.

41

Monegaw Springs

This township was primarily a farming community until the popularity of the springs thrust it into the forefront as a tourist destination. It was believed that the water of the sulphur springs were very therapeutic and people came from miles around, from as far away as Kansas City, to bath in and drink the water in the springs. The waters of of the sulphur springs were very therapeutic and people came from miles around, from as far away as Kansas City, to bathe in and drink the water of the springs. The waters of the springs were thought to be the 'cure all' for any ailment and were highly advertised. People would come, pitch a tent and stay for a week or two at a time to enjoy the springs. For this reason the township had a population of 1440 people.

On the top of a large hill in the northern part of the town stood the log building known as the Monegaw Hotel. This was a three story structure with sleeping rooms on the two upper floors. The ground floor housed an office, dining room and a post office. The building was made in the "dog trot" style, by constructing four individual log buildings with a breezeway running between them. A single roof covered the entire building.

The hotel, like the entire community, maintained a constant "carnival" like atmosphere to entertain the public. Dances were held with regularity to entertain the tourists and many locals joined in on the festivities.

The hotel was a tourist destination itself and the food in the restaurant was known as "top shelf." Missouri McFerrin, the daughter of 'Aunt Hannah McFerrin," was the cook and her reputation as the best cook in the county was known far and wide. She was not only known for her culinary abilities, but also for her hot temper. Anyone who entered her kitchen uninvited or otherwise and aroused her ire might with a flying fry pan.

The beer, wine and whiskey at Monegaw was also 'top shelf' and there was plenty of it served in the town to the vacationing public.

Monegaw Hotel

Montgomery

Sometimes known as the McFerrin Negro settlement, the community of Montgomery was located about three miles southeast of Monegaw Springs just off the Chalk Road to the east.

The Chalk Road ran from Roscoe to Chalk Level and the road to Monegaw Springs branched off a little to the north at the "forks."

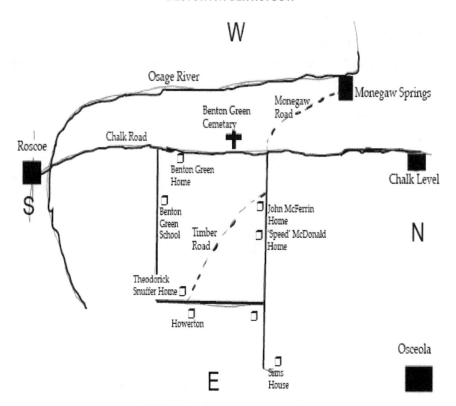

Montgomery Community

People from Montgomery found employment either in Roscoe, three miles away, working on the docks and in the warehouses or in Monegaw Springs catering to the needs of the many tourists that flocked to the area.

John McFerrin, a prominent Negro citizen of Montgomery, had a two story log home with a lean-to on the side, the largest home in the Montgomery settlement. John's wife, known as 'Aunt Hannah,' was fond of all the Youngers because her sister had worked for the family in Jackson County. They were always welcomed in her home and stayed there on many occasions. Aunt Hannah's well-known persimmon beer made her home especially inviting.

Just east of Aunt Hannah's house lived one of her

daughters whose husband was George "Speed" McDonald. Another daughter lived less than three hundred feet to the north. This daughter was married to a mulatto named Wes Brown. Brown was considered to be a 'well-to-do' Negro. He had a nice home setting up on a slight hill.

John and Hannah's son, John Rod McFerrin lived just south of his parents on the same section.

One of the Younger boys' favorite hide-outs was the caves along the Osage River near Monegaw. The caves at Monegaw are situated so that when the Youngers were there, they could look out and survey the countryside in all directions. No one could approach without being easily seen and possibly shot.

George "Speed" McDonald, a son-in-law of Aunt Hannah's (not a member of the gang) had a close relationship with the Youngers and acted as their lookout and cook while they were hiding out in the cave.

"Speed" was also well known for his culinary abilities. When the "Old Soldiers" reunions were held, "Speed" was called upon as head cook and lived to an old age.

There is a story that tells that Cole Younger was sleeping in a room near a window at the McFerrin house. He carved his initials into the window glass with his diamond ring. In later years, lots of folks tried to to buy that window pane from Aunt Hannah, but she declined. The night after she died, that window pane mysteriously disappeared.

Three white families of note lived in or very near the Montgomery settlement. To the north on the Chalk Road lived the John Davis family. The Youngers were well known to the Davises as they rode past their house frequently in their travels and occasionally stopped to pass the time of day.

Just down the Chalk Road to the south, on the east side, was the home of Benton Green, a man who had ridden alongside of Cole Younger at the Battle of Lone Jack, and at the end of the road, after a turn to the north from the Benton Green School lane was the home of Theodrick Snuffer, a long time family friend.

Chapter 7

The Outlaw Trail

In January 1874, Marshal Cobb of Appleton City in St. Clair County led a posse in an effort to capture the well known and notorious Younger brothers.

The Marshal had it on good authority that the boys were either in Monegaw Springs or in the black community of Montgomery. Which ever the case, he was determined that he would capture them and bring them to justice.

It had been a long grueling ride from Appleton City and as the Marshal and his men shared a tin cup of drinking water at the old sulphur spring, a quiet, yet stern voice from behind a large oak tree bid them to put their hands up and stand in a row.

They were relieved of their weapons and sent on their way.

The Youngers had been warned of the impending arrival of the posse before it was half way to Monegaw Springs. Unlike Jesse James, the Youngers were hesitant to take anyone's life.

Chapter 8

Detective Work

After two weeks in the field with their posse, Captain Lull sent the posse home by train from the Clinton, Missouri station to Chicago and he and detective Wright rode south to Osceola.

Upon reaching Osceola on March 15, they checked in to the Commercial Hotel where they assumed the identity of cattle buyers, Wright using his real name as he had served in the Confederate Army with men from St. Clair County and Captain Lull using the alias of W. J. Allen for fear someone might recognize his name as being a known Pinkerton man.

Commercial Hotel, Osceola

As cattle buyers they could move freely about and engage people in all kinds of conversations.

The Younger boys were one of the main topics of the "Spit and Whittle" crowd of old men that loafed around the courthouse square. Lull and Wright took this opportunity to listen and ask questions. It didn't take long for them to discover that the boys were hanging around either the black settlement of Montgomery or at the Snuffer place.

They went to the county Sheriff, a ma named Johnson and asked for his help in procuring a guide that was familiar with the Osage River basin. The Sheriff recommended Edwin B. Daniels, a youngster who had been a deputy from time to time. A young man of 23 years, he was familiar with all of the back roads and wooded areas of the country.

On March 16th they left Osceola, crossed the Osage River and entered Roscoe late in the evening. They checked into the Roscoe House, a two story clap board building on the east side of Main Street. The owner of this establishment was Oliver Burch, a former running mate of Cole Younger who had ridden with Quantrill during the war. As a result, the detectives did not mention the name Younger. Instead, they asked around for the likelihood of anyone having cows for sale in the area.

When it was learned that a widow by the name of Sims, a neighbor of Theodrick Snuffer, had stock she was trying to sell, this was the answer they had been looking for. It would give them the perfect reason for being in the area if anyone asked.

Just after noon, the three men left Roscoe headed north on the Chalk Road. After little more than two miles, they turned east down a narrow dirt road. They passed the new Benton Green School. The land had been donated by Theodrick Snuffer, who did not want the school named after him.

When the men reached the corner where the road led directly past Snuffer's home, Wright elected to fall back and catch up to the others a little farther down the road. He was quite concerned that he might be recognized.

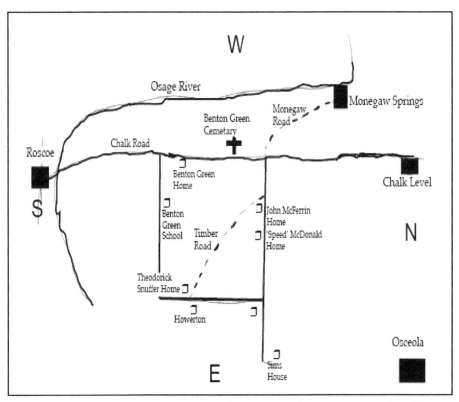

A hundred yards down the road they found the home of Theodrick Snuffer. The two men, Lull and Daniels reined their horses to a stop in the front yard of Snuffer's house.

Snuffer hesitated about going outside until he heard a hail from the front of the house. "Any one home?" Captain Lull called.

Snuffer slowly opened the door and walked outside toward his visitors. Lull was just stepping down from his saddle. "Sir, could you direct us to the Sims' place?" Captain Lull asked.

"You mean the Colonel Sims place?" Snuffer replied.

Chapter 9

March 17, 1874

John Younger was now 23 years old, a delightful young man by all accounts, although a little hot tempered. He had been in a shooting scrape in Texas during 1871 in which he had killed a deputy sheriff. He too, was wounded and went to California to convalesce in the care of his uncle, Coleman L. Younger. Returning to Missouri in late 1873, he was in time to participate in the Gad's Hill robbery, or at least be blamed for it.

John Younger

Jim Younger had turned 26 in January. A veteran of the Civil War, he had ridden with his older brother, Cole, under the command of William Clarke Quantrill during the bushwhacker raid on Lawrence, Kansas, August 21, 1863.

Jim Younger

Jim and John had been making their residence at Aunt Hannah's house for the last week, enjoying a holiday before going south to Arkansas to meet up with brothers, Cole and Bob.

On the night of Tuesday, March 16, the boys attended a dance at the Monegaw Hotel. Both were young, handsome and single. They were the object of the affections of many a young woman at the dance. They had their pick, made their choice and enjoyed the ladies' company. They danced and drank plenty of liquor which was flowing during the dance.

After the dance they returned to the black community of Montgomery and went to the home of John McFerrin where they had been in residence and slept late into the morning of March 17.

Aunt Hannah in later years.

At about 1 p.m. the youngers rode off to Theodrick Snuffer's house, tied their horses behind the shed and went inside for lunch. It was about 2 in the afternoon when they finally settled at the table for the mid-day meal.

The sound of approaching horses in the front yard got their attention. "Theodrick, you better see who that is," said John. "Jim and I will go up in the attic."

"Yeah," said Snuffer turning toward the door.
The boys climbed the ladder through the hole in the ceiling and stationed themselves in such a way as to see through a crack between the logs down into the front yard.
Snuffer waited by the door until he heard the rustling in the ceiling stop.

A voice from outside hailed the house. "Any one home?"

Snuffer opened the door and stepped outside just as Captain Lull was stepping to the ground from his mount.

"Sir, can you direct us to the Sims' place?" Lull asked.

"You mean the Colonel Sims' place?" Snuffer inquired.

"We were told that the widow, Mrs. Sims, has some cattle to sell and that's the place we would like to find."

Snuffer thought they meant the Sims that lived about a mile from Monegaw Springs and went on to give detailed instructions on how to get there.

Ed Daniels kept silent during the exchange and Wright rode by and pulled off into a wooded area just out of sight.

Lull remounted his horse and he and Daniels rode out of the gate following Wright.

Snuffer came back into the house as the boys were coming down the ladder from the attic.

"What do you make of that, Theodrick?" Jim aked.

"I dunno, but they didn't go by the directions I gave them."

Jim sast down at the table and broke a piece of bread.

He was happy to go on with his meal.

John, the youngest, more excitable and more suspicious brother, spoke. "Jim, did you see that fellow that was on his horse? I swear he was acting nervous as a polecat on a hot rock."

"I didn't notice him being nervous," said Jim. "He was just looking around."

"Yeah," said John. "his head was moving real slow as he looked around, but did you notice his fingers? They never stopped moving, and he kept his hand close to his pistol."

"That's no reason to think they're the law," said Jim.

"Did you see the hardware they were packing?" John asked. "No roving cattle buyer would be carrying guns like that. They were too well armed to be mere cattle buyers."

John picked up his double barreled shotgun that had been leaning next to the table. "Let's go after them and find out if they're the law or cattle buyers."

"No. Let them go. There's no use asking for trouble, Jim said.

Following John as he scurried out the door, the boys rushed back to the shed, mounted their horses and galloped off in the direction the strangers had taken.

There would be witnesses on this warm spring afternoon.

Captain Lull and E. B. Daniels were riding together with detective Wright riding some twenty yards ahead. They were now within the confines of the Montgomery community.

George "Speed" McDonald's wif had given birth that very morning with Granny Sims acting as midwife. He was outside splitting kindling for the cook stove for Granny Sims.

Two hundred feet away from the riders was the rail fence that surrounded the home of John Davis. His son, Ol, fifteen, was wielding a small axe, cutting sprouts from the fence.

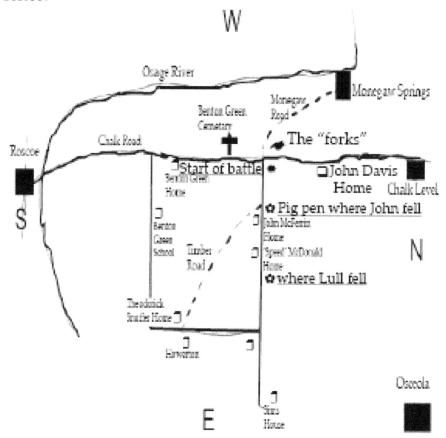

It was now two-thirty in the afternoon. Captain Lull and Ed Daniels rode along together at a slow gait with Wright still twenty to thirty yards ahead.

Fast moving hoofbeats caused Lull to look around. The Younger boys were upon them, John carrying his barreled shotgun aimed directly at him. Jim had one of his pistols out of its holster holding it in the 'ready to fire' position.

Captain Lull and Ed Daniels reined up and held still.

Jim called to Wright, "You there, hold up!"

Wright put the spurs to his horse and he bolted westward toward the forks. Jim fired his pistol and Wright's hat went spinning off to the ground.

John kept his shotgun on Lull and Daniels as Wright galloped away.

John ordered Lull and Daniels to drop their guns, which they did.

Jim stepped from his saddle an picked up the Pinkerton's revolver. It was company issue, an English .43 caliber Tranter double action revolver with a $5^7/_8$ inch barrel.

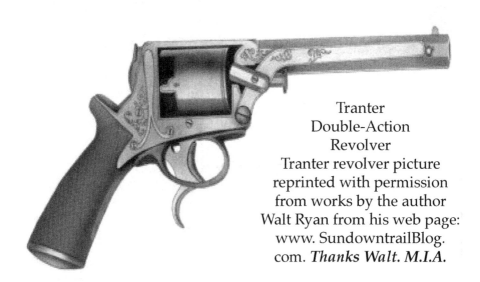

Tranter
Double-Action
Revolver
Tranter revolver picture reprinted with permission from works by the author Walt Ryan from his web page: www. SundowntrailBlog. com. *Thanks Walt. M.I.A.*

"Where you fellas from?" John demanded.

"Osceola." Lull answered.

"What are you doing here?"

"You sure you're not detectives looking for someone? I believe I've seen one of you at Monegaw Springs," said John.

"No!" Daniels pleaded. "My name is E. B. Daniels and I can prove who I am and where I'm from."

John glanced at the guns on the ground. "Then, why in hell are you carrying all these sidearms?"

"Good God," said Daniels. "Doesn't every man traveling through this country carry guns, and besides, don't I have as much right to carry a gun as anyone?"

"That's enough of that," answered John. "Let's not have any of that smart talk."

Jim was just mounting his horse with Lull and Daniels' guns. "John, these are damn fine guns. It's sure nice of these boys to make us a present of them."

John was distracted, looking at the gun Jim was tucking into his belt when Captain Lull reached under his cape, behind his back and pulled out a gun he had hidden, a Number 2 Smith & Wesson revolver. He aimed at John and fired.

Smith & Wesson No. 2 revolver
Picture reprinted with permission from works by the author Walt Ryan from his web page: www.SundowntrailBlog.com. *Thanks Walt, M.I.A.*

The bullet struck John in the neck passing upward. The report from the gun held by Lull caused his horse to jump sideways.

Although he was wounded, John managed to air his shotgun at Lull and fire, the blast striking his left arm and shoulder. Some of the BBs may have hit his horse because it spun and bolted into the brush at the side of the road.

John, still abler to ride, urged his horse forward and shot twice at Lull with his pistol, the first bullet missing and the second passing through his left lung. He slumped from his frightened horse which was attempting to run away through the brush and fell beside the road.

At the sound of Lulls gun, Daniels put the spurs to his horse and attempted to flee, but Jim's Navy Colt spoke death, the bullet striking him in the neck. He was dead before he hit the ground.

.44 Caliber Navy Colt

Wobbling sideways in the saddle, John looked over at his older brother. He was dead. He slumped forward and rolled from his horse. As he fell, he went over a low fence into John McFerrin's hog pen.

Knowing his brother was dead, Jim stepped into the hog pen and removed his brother's pistols, watch and other personal affects. He heard a noise and looked up to see George "Speed" McDonald standing nearby. He handed Speed one of the pistols and instructed him to catch up a horse and go tell Theodrick Snuffer what had happened.

McDonald sent another Negro to tell Snuffer and returned to the hog pen to stand guard over John's body until help arrived to remove it.

Jim caught his horse and rode off in the direction that the escaping Wright had taken. When he was unable to find him, he turned back to Snuffer's place to tell ;him what had happened and to make arrangements for the car of John's body. After a meeting with Snuffer, Jim mounted his horse and rode south into Arkansas to join his brother, Cole and Bob.

Ol Davis ran and told his father that he had heard shots and saw a man fall from his horse. Mr. Davis immediately walked down the road to where the gun battle had taken place and found Daniels face down in the mud. He came upon Captain Lull who had pulled himself across the road and was sitting up against a tree.

Approaching Lull, Mr. Davis said, "Looks like you have some trouble."

In a pleading tone Lull said, "I hope I have fallen into good hands, Sir."

Davis smiled at the injured man, saying, "I can assure you that I will not harm a hair on you head."

Aunt Hannah prepared a pallet on her porch where Captain Lull was laid until his wounds could be seared with a hot poker to stop the bleeding and then he was brought into the house and laid in the same room where John Younger's body lay.

A rider was sent to Osceola to tell Sheriff James R. Johnson what had happened.

Meanwhile, Detective Wright had ridden to Osceola and reported to Sheriff Johnson that Lull and Daniels had been shot and maybe killed by two men who came upon them on the road in the community of Montgomery.

A posse was formed that started for Montgomery, but when they met a rider from the battle scene with the news that Daniels was dead and Lull wounded, they returned to Osceola.

Soon a rider arrived from Roscoe and told the Sheriff that Lull and the body of Daniels had been taken to Roscoe. A second posse, led by a deputy, took a wagon to retrieve Daniels's body and went to Roscoe.

When the posse reached Roscoe, about five in the afternoon, they were told by Dr. Marquis that Lull was suffering from a broken left arm full of buckshot and a pistol ball wound that had passed through his left lung.

⭐ Marks the room where Lull was kept.

Chapter 10

The Vigil

David Crowder

David Crowder, a youngster of seventeen years and a resident of Roscoe was upset by the news of the shootings. He immediately rode out to Montgomery to look in on his wife-to-be, Emma Davis.

With the possibility of revenge being taken on John Younger's body by friends of Ed Daniels, David was asked to spend the night standing watch over the body. It was not unusual in those days for the body of an outlaw to be hanged from a tree for sight-seers to gawk at.

As night fell, David sat in the darkened room next to John's body, a shotgun across his lap, keeping guard.

About nine in the evening a young woman entered the cabin, a pistol on her hip. She did not say a word to David but paced up and down until the break of day when she left as quietly as she had arrived. It has always been thought that the young woman was the Younger boys' sister, Henrietta, who thought highly of her brothers.

The following day, John's body was taken to Theodrick Snuffer's place and buried beneath a large cedar tree, brush being placed over the grave to disguise the disturbed earth.

That evening it was decided that John's body should be buried in the old Yeater Cemetery a few miles to the southeast on the south side of Chalk Level to Osceola road.

With help from Theodrick Snuffer, George "Speed" McDonald placed John's body into his wagon and took the long trip to Yeater Cemetery.

"Speed" dug the grave at an angle so that it could be easily identified in the future and buried John, his head pointing northwest and his feet to the southeast. For two weeks after, the grave was closely guarded by friends including Granny Sims. As a result, the depression of John's grave can be identified today. A stone has been placed on the site in recent years.

Chapter 11

The Aftermath

Edwin B. Daniels was buried in Osceola at the highest point in the cemetery. The entire community felt the loss of this young man.

Edwin B. Daniels Tombstone

On March 18, 1874, a coroner's inquest was held and the verdict was as follows:

"We, the jury, find that John Younger came to his death by a pistol shot, supposed to be in the hands of W. J. Allen (the alias of Captain Lull). We, the jury, also find that Edwin B. Daniels came to his death by a pistol shot, supposed to have been fired by the hand of James Younger."

William Pinkerton arrived in Roscoe, bringing with him, Marian B. Lull, the wife of the wounded man. She joined him in the northwest room of the upstairs in the Roscoe House. She was in a state of anxiety because of all the theaters running plays about how the James gang was getting the better of the Pinkerton agency. She sat bravely by his side although he was conscious and most of his sleep was fitful.

Lull's health seemed to be declining, so Dr. Marquis transported him to Osceola and called on Dr. McNeill of that town. Dr. McNeill, a Confederate veteran surgeon of the Civil War, had great experience with gunshot wounds and it was now believed that Captain Lull would recover.

On April 9, 1874, it was announced that Captain Lull had suddenly taken a turn for the worse and died. He was placed into a casket and transported by wagon to the train depot in Clinton, Missouri, twenty-five miles to the north, where his body was sent back to Chicago.

This may not be true...

The following is an excerpt from the book by Wilbur A. Zink of Appleton City, Missouri "THE ROSCOE GUN BATTLE - YOUNGER BROTHERS VS. PINKERTON DETECTIVES. Copyright 1967, Democrat Publishing Co. Inc.

One evening Dr. McNeill came to the Nesbit (a lawyer) home to seek assistance from his friend.

Mr. Nesbit's son, Charles F. Nesbit, was a young man at the time and he later wrote a family history book entitled, "An American Family" which was published in 1932. He tells of the former Confederate Army surgeon's visit this way:

One evening while I as at home playing, my father opened the door in response to a knock, and I saw Dr. McNeill with his long white beard. He was the big doctor of the section. He had been a surgeon in the Confederate Army and went all through the war. I knew of no one sick and could not understand his coming. He sat down and began to talk to my father, "Frank, what will happen to me if I say a man is dead who isn't dead?"

"Well," replied my father, laughing, "doctors often make mistakes, but I didn't know they made them as bad as that."

Dr. McNeill said, "But I am serious about this. It is no laughing matter, Frank."

Dr. McNeill

My father asked me to leave the room. I did go out of the room, but I was very careful to leave a crack in the door and put my ear to it. The doctor explained the situation. "You know that Pinkerton detective who was shot when John Younger was killed? Well, he is going to get well. But the Youngers and their friends have indicated that he will never leave the the county alive. It is twenty-five miles to the nearest railroad and I do not think he will ever get to it if he starts. Now, the Pinkerton Agency at Chicago has sent a detective down here and they want me to say that he is dead, and ship him out in a coffin. It is the only way we will ever get him out, but I don't know what to do."

The doctor was an honest man but he kept remembering his promise to save life. This, not doubt, is the reason he considered such a move.

"Well," my father answered, "I don't think it will hurt. Doctors often make mistakes and if you can stand making a mistake like saying a man is dead when he isn't, I don't see that anybody can do anything about it."

The next week the paper stated that the detective was very low and much worse and that Dr. McNeill didn't think he would get well. A few days later a notice appeared that he had died. He was put in a coffin and carried in a farm wagon to Clinton, Missouri. The casket was put in the baggage car and after the train started, the Pinkerton detective (Captain Lull) got out and got away to Chicago.

✳✳✳

Dr. McNeill had a daughter named Cora L. McNeill and in 1898 she published a book entitled, "Mizzoura." It was the only book at this time written about the Youngers that had been sanctioned by them. She made many visits to Stillwater, Minnesota, to visit Cole and Jim in prison and corresponded with them freely. In her book she also leaves no doubt that the Pinkerton Detective Lull did not die but arose from the coffin.

Today a monument marks the place where the battle took place. The old McFerrin log cabin where John Younger lay in silent death still stands erect as if it does not want to give up its story. The old log house where David Crowder later moved, just a quarter of a mile east, is in part still there. Only a grove of trees marks the spot where John Davis lived. The old Snuffer place, where John and Jim spent their last few happy moments, is now only a memory...

The Old Roscoe Gun Battle Monument

New
Gun
Battle
Monument

About The Authors

Meredith I. Anderson, author, historian and licensed Chef's Aid, was born in Osceola, Missouri. A graduate of Weber State University in Ogden, Utah, he was the president of the state wide organization, League of Utah Writers in 2007. His book, **MORE THAN A JOB, AN ADVENTURE** won the coveted Gold Quill for Literature Award. This book is available on Amazon.com, createspace.com, Barnes & Noble and Kindle. This book is also an audio book available from Audible.com and itunes. A Vietnam veteran, Meredith left active duty with the Navy as a Storekeeper Second Class (E5). He has spent the last forty years as a journalist, writing magazine and newspaper columns about fishing, hunting, camping and cooking to entertain the outdoor enthusiast. He makes his home with his wife of 49 years in Osceola.

Linda Pool Anderson, novelist and historian, has released her newest Trilogy, **They Were Lawmen: The Outlaw Trail** is the first book. A graduate of the University of Utah, she is a retired commercial airline pilot and Director of Flight Operations for the third largest regional freight airline in the US. They flew mail and UPS throughout the Rocky Mountain West.

THEY WERE
LAWMEN:THE
OUTLAW TRAIL

LINDA POOL ANDERSON

The Story of two brothers, Charles and Abel Barnhill, who rode out of Fort Smith, Arkansas into the badlands of Indian Territory in pursuit of outlaws, murderers, thieves and bootleggers for the court of Judge Isaac Parker, the hanging judge.

Written from court records, newspapers and journals from the time, this book was three years in research and two years in writing and publication. *A Great Read...*

Some books by these authors:

Not a war story, but the story of a young man's adventures during a time of war. Follow Pete from a catastrophic mining disaster in Utah to the rolling deck of an American "Man of War."

He told his mining boss, "I'm going to get a job where they won't have to dig me up to bury me." And so, the story begins and becomes a page turning adventure that you can enjoy.

After the Civil War, the Indian Territory became a sanctuary for villains seeking refuge from the laws of their native state. At the time, the law of the land was written in such a manner as to prevent non-Indian outlaws from being arrested or prosecuted by Indian courts. As a result, the Indian Territory was the perfect place for ruthless men escaping justice to hide.

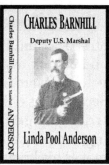

A collection of thirteen short stories about young women, ages 11 to 24. Each story is from newspaper clippings, reports and letters written during America's greatest conflict. Yes, the true events have been fictionalized somewhat to give the characters personality and voice. This book is designed especially for readers, grade 8 and above. This version of this book is currently being used by a local university as recommended reading in their History Department.

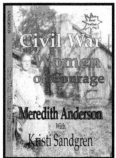

The American Civil War, one of the most violent wars ever contested, started in reality in 1850, when the Compromise of 1850 deposed the Missouri Compromise of 1820 and made **"Popular Vote,"** the way by which the decision would be made, to designate a state FREE or SLAVE.

Kansas became the test, northerners and southerner both pouring into the territory, voting to make that new state what either side preferred. Soon,

bands of armed men rode through Kansas and Missouri, most from the anti-slavery north, the 'Red Legs' and 'Jayhawkers.' Other bands, representing the pro-slavery point of view, rode in from Missouri. These "border ruffians," soon known as 'bushwhackers,' like the 'Red Legs,' killed and burned out people with an opposite point of view.

The stories written in this book are typical of those found throughout history. The explorers of the Old World discovered a continent that was new to them and they jabbed their flag into the ground and claimed that land for their sovereign. There was no regard for the native peoples of that land.

At first, welcoming the Spanish, Dutch, Portuguese, French and English onto their shores, the Indians soon discovered that the strangers in their land were not there to live peacefully beside the Indian. The newcomers' interests lay in taking the riches of The New World back to their home country, controlling the land and dominating and subduing the native people.

When war broke out between two white factions, many times the Indians chose the losing side because they were promised the return of their lands if they won. When the wars were over, the white losers were banished back to where they came from while the Indian was more feared and hated than ever before.

The story of twelve year-old Annie Jewel Bounds, taken from letters and publications of the time. Annie would have gone off to war with her father, but when he was lost in battle, she convinces her mother to allow her to dress as a Yankee drummer boy and march off with a unit that is scheduled for discharge in just six weeks.

Her adventure places her in the thick of the fire and smoke at the Battle of Wilson's Creek, a few miles from Springfield, Missouri. Fought on August 10, 1861, it is the first 'real' battle of the Civil War., sometimes labelled the 'Bull Run' of the west. The 'Battle of Oak Hill,' as it was called by the Confederates, was a victory for the south. The better armed, trained and equipped Union Army lost a quarter of their forces against a foe twice their size.

Hearing the hoofbeats of twenty horses entering the yard at the front of her house, Mattea pulled the lead rope, releasing the cow she was milking and ran into the house to find five Sioux braves wearing war paint sitting at her table, smoking her husband's tobacco from the humidor on the mantle.

Mattea repressed her anger and shock. "Cinder Horse, why have you come to my home? And coming in without being invited." "Remember," he said in a stern voice, "do not go near the lodges of the settlement! Do not go near the Post Road and do not give an alarm or you and your children will die." He prodded her with the tip of his war lance. "Go! Go to your mother!"

You can order an autographed copy of any of the books written by Meredith and Linda Anderson and you won't have to pay the list price.

Simply mark the order form on the next page and send check or money order to the authors at:

Make checks payable to:

L & M Anderson
825 Outer Lyons Private Road
Osceola, MO 64776

Phone: 417-664-0012
Email: Linda
linda.skymama@gmail.com
          Andy
fisherman.anderson@juno.com

Many of our books are also available as **Audiobooks.**
   They are available from **Audible.com,**
   Amazon.com, and **itunes.**

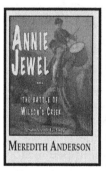   

You can order any of these books at a special price by filling out the order form on the opposite page. ☞

   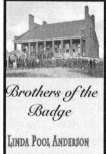

Order Form

Title	RETAIL	Price	order QTY
Annie Jewel and The Battle. of Wilson's Creek	16.99	10.00	
Bushwhackers of Missouri. and General Order 11	16.99	10.00	
Fire Hair.	16.99	10.00	
General Order Eleven, 1863 .	16.99	10.00	
Ozarkia Cooking...	16.99	10.00	
Ozarkia Cooking 2...	16.99	10.00	
Times... They're a changin'....	16.99	10.00	
Uprising	16.99	10.00	
University Edition, Civil War Women of Courage	16.99	10.00	
Guns of Monegaw and the Roscoe Gun Battle	16.99	10.00	
Civil War Women of Courage...	18.99	12.00	
Vietnam Edition, More Than. a Job, An Adventure	16.99	10.00	
Whispering Oaks 2, Unexpected Adventures	16.99	10.00	
Whispering Oaks, The Curse..	16.99	10.00	
More Than a Job, An Adventure	21.99	15.00	
Author: Linda Anderson			
They were Lawmen: The outlaw trail...	16.99	**10.00**	
Brothers of the Badge	16.99	**10.00**	
Killers on the loose	1699	10.00	
Charles Barnhill, Deputy US Marshal	24.99	20.00	

Order $_____

Add $3 for the first book and $2 for each
additional book for Shipping & Handling .... $_____

Note to Author: Sign dedication to: **Total Order $**_____

_____

👉) Cut along dotted line.

L & M Anderson
825 Outer Lyons Private Road
Osceola, MO 64776

MATTEA AND THE SIOUX

As a special treat for the reader, the author invites you to read this story from his book "CIVIL WAR, WOMEN OF COURAGE"--- I hope you enjoy it. Thank You..
Meredith Anderson

It was one of those lovely spring days in early May on the southwestern Minnesota frontier. The beauty of the season was at its best. Michael whistled a tune as he walked behind his horse watching the blade of his plow break the sod. Birds sang in the trees, a cottontail rabbit hopped into a thicket at the edge of the forest as a squirrel chased its mate around the base of a large walnut tree.

Michael Prine had come west with his family to farm the new country. He was plowing the ground that would soon be his cornfield. The deep fertile soil turned easily under his plow as he walked behind his team of horses.

Michael was a full year out of his indentured contract. He and his wife, Elizabeth, had left England where he was a shoe-maker, and she a seamstress. Sponsored by a family of wealthy clothiers in New York, they had worked for three years in their sponsor's shops making clothing and boots for the people of the city. Their sponsor had given Michael and Elizabeth their contracts eighteen months earlier as a Christmas present.

Their sponsor hoped the Prines would remain with the busi-ness and make their home in New York, but Michael had heard stories of land that was yours for the asking along the frontier. He wanted to build a new life for himself and his family.

Michael, Elizabeth and their children had come west to New Ulm, Minnesota with several other immigrant families.

As winter ended, Michael and his family left New Ulm and

went further west, to the northern end of Sheteck Lake. He had been on his place for two months and still lived out of his wagon and a makeshift lean-to, working the land and getting it ready for planting. Today, the turning of his fields would be finished. Next would be the planting of corn, squash and potatoes.

Elizabeth was in the shade of the lean-to cooking squirrels Michael had snared the day before. His two daughters, who had been helping him, ran down to the creek to play. The creek was swollen from spring runoff. He had cautioned his girls not to go too close to the swollen torrent which would certainly drown them.

Michael plodded along behind his team enjoying the scent of the newly turned earth. The screaming of his children interrupted his plowing.

Mattea, his youngest, came to the edge of the clearing sixty yards from Michael. "Papa, Papa! Help!" she cried and darted back toward the stream. His heart sank. In one motion he pulled the team to a stop, dropped the reins and jerked his rucksack off his shoulders. He ran as fast as he could, across the open field to the path through the trees.

At the grove of trees, the path broke left, he could see his girls standing on the edge of the bank trying to reach a small boy clinging to a log. The log had jammed against a fallen tree, and the boy was barely hanging on. Michael jumped down to the stream's edge and reached the youngster, pulling him to shore near the girls. It was an Indian boy about the same age as his eldest daughter, Ruth, who was going to be twelve in August.

Michael slumped down on one elbow beside the motionless boy. Running to the boy's aid had been exhausting.

Pressing against her father's shoulder to get a better view, Ruth asked, "Who is he, Father?"

Michael's heavy breathing had slowed. "He's one of our red neighbors."

"Red?" Mattea looked more closely. The boy's body was nearly purple from the frigid water. "He looks more like a cinder to me."

Michael swept him up in his large arms to carry him back to the family camp. Ruth and Mattea ran ahead.

Ruth arrived first. "Mama, Father is bringing a red boy he fished out of the crick."

Mattea now arrived, rendering her opinion. "He's not really red, Mama. He's 'cinder-colored.' He's more the color of a burnt stick than a red man."

By the time Michael reached camp, Elizabeth had towels and warm blankets ready to receive the youngster.

The boy, cold and exhausted from his ordeal, fell asleep and slept well into the evening. He awoke as the sun was going down. He sat up, wrapping his blankets tightly to his body and looked with wide eyes at the strangers. Mattea gave him a cup of warm soup which he quickly drank. He reached out and touched Mattea's flowing red hair as she knelt to hand him a second cup of soup and a piece of bread. "Fire Hair," he said, taking the food. After eating the bread and drinking the soup, he laid the cup aside, curled up and went to sleep.

The next morning the family gathered around the breakfast table under the lean-to. Work assignments had been given out and the meal of bacon, eggs and potatoes was almost over.

Mattea noticed him first. The impetuous little red-headed girl held out her index finger, pointing at the boy standing behind her father's chair. "Look! It's Cinder. He looks a lot better today."

Mr. Prine, half turned in his chair. Michael looked at the boy he had pulled from the raging stream. He was not a little boy at all, but a young man, about twelve or thirteen. In the Indian world, he would be choosing a name and going through the rites of manhood very soon. "Come join us for breakfast. Come now, have some food." He smiled and made eating gestures with his hands as he motioned the boy to the table.

The boy sat down. Mattea set a plate heaped with fried potatoes, bread, bacon and eggs in front of him. The youth smiled at Michael, picked up his butter knife and began to eat. Soon he had sopped the last bit of egg with his bread and leaned back, drinking a cup of honey-sweetened coffee. Ruth brought a cup of milk for the young man, but Michael motioned her away. "Indians don't drink milk because it can make them very sick," he said.

"I'd sure like to know what you were doing in that creek," Michael mused as he lit his pipe, not expecting a reply.

"I fall in water at crossing," was the boy's answer.

Michael's jaw dropped. "What? You speak English?"

"Yes. I have three tongues." The youngster, beamed with confidence.

"Do tell," said Michael, shifting his chair to look the boy square in the face.

"The white eyes have been in this land since the time of my father's father. Maybe before that. At first, they walked with the people and were friends of the people. There was the time of great war with peoples against peoples. Then there was a time before my father when white men came and tried to destroy the people, but the people ran away to their strongholds in the black hills of the Dakotah."

"Now is a quiet time." The boy sipped at his coffee. "My people have come for a season of hunting and gathering. Our chiefs have sat at the fires of counsel all winter and say white man is not many here. Whites should be avoided. They do not know the people. Our Chiefs have told us they carry disease that kills the people."

Michael and the young Indian talked for another hour. "This is the moon for passing to manhood for me. I will choose a name and be able to accompany the braves of the tribe on hunts and perhaps join in the war against the Blackfeet to the west. I am the best youth in the village with a bow and arrow and second to none as a horseman." He spoke with confidence. "I was thinking of taking the name, 'Spotted Horse,' but after being named 'Cinder' by Little Fire Hair, I may take the name, 'Cinder Horse.'" The table chat was interrupted by the appearance of three Sioux braves standing near the front opening of the lean-to. No one had heard them come up. The dog was off chasing rabbits, and there was no alarm from him.

Michael, recovered from his surprise and motioned the braves to come, sit and join them at the table. The braves stood where they were.

The tallest of the three spoke to the boy in English, "Your grandfather sent us. Come with us."

The boy looked up at the brave as though he was surprised by the refusal of Michael's hospitality. The brave spoke again, "These whites are bad, they make men crazy with liquor and force children to drink milk, and the children die."

Elizabeth reached the crock pitcher half full of milk in the middle of the table and drew it toward her.

The boy slid from his chair, turning to Mattea as he left. "Thank you, Fire Hair," he said as he followed the departing braves. They walked along the edge of the plowed field and into the forest. The whole family watched as more braves, perhaps a dozen, appeared at the edge of the forest and fell in behind the departing group.

Michael picked up his floppy hat, placed it on his head and looked around at his family. "Now, that was an experience."

Elizabeth still had her hand on the milk. "It was a very frightening experience!"

Michael smiled at his wife. "Yes dear, but those are people with great integrity. They don't usually harm anyone unless they are on the warpath."

***

The summer passed slowly. A long warm growing season with adequate rain was producing bountiful crops. The Prines enjoyed fresh corn, beans, squash and even new potatoes. The entire family worked hard during the summer and constructed of a modest log house with a sleeping loft for the girls. They also built a small barn for the cow, a partially covered pig pen and a chicken coop.

One warm afternoon, Michael was hunting in the forest north of his property. He came across the tracks of a large white tail buck. He dismounted and tracked the deer on foot as he often did. He crept through the trees and undergrowth. He sensed he was getting near his prey.

Suddenly, there was a loud *"thud, thud,"* the sound of a star-tled deer getting up from its bedding spot. At the same moment he heard the shrill swish of arrows passing through the air, and the hollow sounding *"bump, bump, bump,"* as they struck their mark.

Michael, on his belly, inched up through the brush to see in the clearing ahead of him.

Four Sioux braves appeared from the undergrowth. In sec-onds the deer's throat was cut and its entrails removed. Leath-er thongs were placed on the deer's legs and it was strung on a pole. What a sight! Michael had hoped he would get a shot at this deer, but it was worth the loss of it to see the Indians harvest it in such an efficient manner. The archery skill of the braves was remarkable. Three shafts had landed behind the deer's left front shoulder within an inch of each other. The big deer had died and fallen almost instantaneously.

Michael's attention was diverted from the activity in the clearing when his horse flinched sideways breaking brush and pulling the reins which were wrapped around his left hand. He turned to see what was spooking his horse and saw a brave with a raised tomahawk. He quickly pulled his flintlock up be-tween himself and the falling blade of the hatchet. The Indian was on him.

Michael kicked upward with both feet as hard as he could. The brave nearly rubbed noses with Michael as he flew over his head. In an instant, both men were on their feet facing each other. The brave raised his tomahawk and was about to charge when a voice from the clearing commanded "Hold!"

The four braves that had been cleaning the deer stood next to the man with the raised tomahawk.

One of the braves spoke in Sioux and the warrior slowly lowered his weapon. "This is the father of 'Little Fire Hair.' He is the white eyes that saved Cinder Horse from drowning three moons ago."

The senior brave extended his hand to Michael. "I am Spot-ted Buffalo. I came to your lodge to get Cinder Horse. We have

82

watched you and your family for much of the season. You work hard. You are a good hunter. We do not wish to harm you. You were tracking this deer. You may have it."

Two of the braves cut the deer free from its pole and heaved it across Michael's saddle.

Michael was overwhelmed, he didn't know exactly what to do or say. He fumbled in his pocket and found his drawstring bag of smoking tobacco. He handed it to Spotted Buffalo. "Thank you for the deer. I'll try not to make a habit of sneaking up on you fellows."

The Indians all tipped their heads courteously and disappeared into the forest. Michael had a fine deer and he hadn't fired a shot!

When Michael reached home and told the story of his meeting with the Sioux, Ruth and Mattea were very excited. To think that the young brave had taken the name that Mattea gave him was very thrilling.

To Elizabeth, it was a nightmare. She had many misgivings about coming to the frontier. She imagined her husband never coming home, lying dead in the forest, or worse yet, captured and tortured by the savages. She was very upset by the whole tale.

***

Harvest season had arrived. There was a bigger harvest than Michael had expected. A second cellar had to be dug for the extra potatoes, onions and carrots. The dried corn was placed in the barn.

The first hard freeze came, signaling the time to slaughter a pig. After hanging and cooling the meat would have to be salted or smoked for winter storage.

In the chilly October morning, Michael went out to the pig pen and selected a large boar, adequate for feeding the family over the winter.

As he built up a large fire for burning the hair off the hog, he saw four horsemen break the brush at the southern end of the cornfield near the creek.

He could tell immediately that they were Sioux. They were coming fast. He looked at the Indians and then at his flintlock lying against the back of the chicken coop. He could reach it, fire one, maybe two shots before they were on top of him. He could see they were all wearing war paint!

By the time he made up his mind to do nothing, the entire band reined their horses to an abrupt halt next to him kicking up clouds of dust. The youngest rider slid from his horse and stood in front of Michael, a brightly colored war shield on his arm. It was Cinder Horse!

Cinder Horse smiled a big grin. "The paint is not for you, Father of Little Fire Hair. We are on our way to fight the Black-feet who are invading our hunting ground to the south in the Dakotah."

Cinder Horse handed Michael the war shield. It was about eighteen inches across, made of buffalo hide strung on willow and adorned with the head of a brightly painted war horse. Locks of fur were at four equal points around the edges, and two eagle feathers hung off the bottom.

"Hang this on your lodge. It will protect you if any of the people pass," said Cinder Horse.

Michael smiled. "Thank you, I have a gift for you, too."

Michael dashed into the house, returning with a large pouch of smoking tobacco. The pouch was red satin, with a striking embroidered crest. "This was a gift for me many years ago. I would like you to have it. It was given to me by a very brave warrior of the King of England."

"Have a good season of the sleeping bear," said Cinder Horse. "We will return to hunt again when the geese fill the sky to the north." He swung up on his horse, and the braves disappeared as quickly as they had arrived.

Michael took the shield and placed it next to the front door.

Many bands of Indians passed the Prine home in the fol-lowing days, some with war paint, but none stopped, none spoke. It was as if an invisible guardian stood watch over their home.

In the spring, the Sioux were back as they had promised, but the family did not see Cinder Horse.

The years passed quickly and Ruth met a young man from Ohio. They were married and moved back to the Ohio River Valley.

It was Mattea's fifteenth year and she was wed to Phineas B. Hurtz, a man of means with a house constructed of sawed lumber bought from the new steam sawmill at the Sheteck Lake settlement. Phineas raised quality horses and sold them all at a good profit. His large farm was neighboring to the south of the Prines, just off the road to New Ulm.

The Prines' benefactors in New York had died in a boating accident, leaving the Prines their stores as well as their fine house. Elizabeth was elated and could not wait to return to civilization. She had enjoyed living on the frontier, but too often, it frightened her and made her long for the security of the city.

Michael on the other hand, loved the wide open and wild frontier, but he knew he would be happy anywhere, as long as his beloved Elizabeth was there. If moving back East would make Elizabeth happy, he was all for it. He owned his homestead. He could sell it to a westward bound immigrant in New York or keep it in the family and give it to one of the many grandchildren that he expected to have.

Phineas agreed to keep an eye on it so that it would not fall into total ruin.

On the day that Michael left the house for the last time, he stood on the porch and touched the Sioux war shield. "Take good care of my things, old friend. You can never tell, I may return one day."

The settlement of Sheteck Lake was growing rapidly. People, particularly German immigrants, were pouring into the area, setting up farms. There were many new businesses, a sawmill, livery, a general store, a church and even a post office.

Mattea's new home was right on the road to New Ulm. From the porch of the Phenias Hurtz farmhouse, Mattea saw practically all of the people traveling into Sheteck Lake from the East and North.

Once a week, the mail carrier, Mr. Johnson, would come through from New Ulm, picking up the mail from the settlement and returning it to the city for transport east. Each time through, he would stop at the Hurtz house to water his horse at the trough near the front gate and chat for a few minutes. Mattea always managed to find a large slice of pie or piece of fried chicken for this friendly traveler.

Every year, the Sioux came in the spring and left after the first freeze of the fall. Mattea had taken great pains to learn the language of the Sioux, to talk to them and trade fairly with them. She had often told her husband, Phineas, "If you don't trade fairly with them, they will steal whatever they want."

Every week, when the post rider came, he brought news, and an occasional newspaper, telling of the disturbing events taking place in the east. The country was in a state of agitation over states rights and slavery.

Mattea's mother wrote:

Your father is involved in a business venture to establish a factory to sew uniforms and make boots for the Union Army. We are prospering beyond our fondest hopes. I can sleep at night without the fear of being scalped in my sleep. There are some disadvantages too. The air is filled with wood smoke from cook stoves and soot that drifts down from coal burning chimneys and coats everything...

Mattea had never seen a black man until she married Phineas. He had a constant companion named Moses, a runaway slave who came on to his place several years before. Phenias had treated him kindly, and he stayed and became a member of the Hurtz family. He lived in a back room off the kitchen and was a great contributor to the farm and the family. He was a farmer and understood horses, livestock and preserving food.

Mr. Hurtz also had a stable boy, Joshua, who ate his meals with the family. Joshua, seventeen, lived in a room in the barn during the summer. In the winter he slept on a bunk in Moses' room. He was another runaway. He had run away at the age of fourteen from an orphanage in the east. He had bummed his way across the country until he reached the Hurtz farm where he stopped to water the old horse he was riding. Phenias invited him in for a meal, and he just stayed. He was good with horses and enjoyed working on the farm. He worked hard and was always pleasant.

Joshua met a young woman at the settlement of Sheteck Lake named Jeanie O'brian. Her father was the blacksmith of the village. Joshua met her when he went with Phenias on a horse trading day. They had been going to church socials together ever since and were talking about getting married.

Mattea had two children. Phillip had just turned three, and Josie would be one year old in September.

One cool May morning in 1862 a Troop of US Calvary and mounted infantry came past the front of the Hurtz place. The long column consisted of troops, wagons, livestock and cannons. Two officers reined their horses through the gate, tied them up to the hitching post, walked to the front porch and knocked.

Mattea opened the door to find a tall bearded young captain on her porch with a younger lieutenant standing behind him. The captain held the cuffed leather riding glove from his right hand in his left. He stood a little taller as Mattea opened the door wide. He removed his wide brimmed hat with his right hand. "Ma'am," a heavy Pennsylvania accent came forth, "we understand that this is the home of Phenias Hurtz, the horseman."

"That's correct," she said with a wry smile. "What can we do for you?"

"We're here on official business, Ma'am. If you would be so kind as to call Mr. Hurtz for us," he said in a friendly tone.

Phenias, Joshua and Moses were down at the barn shoeing horses so Mattea went to the large triangle bell hung from a porch rafter and rang it with a couple of quick clockwise motions, waited a few seconds and then struck it again, with two single chimes.

The prearranged signal told Phenias that he had company on the front porch and that there were two visitors. He grabbed his pistol from his work bench in the barn, shoved the barrel into his pocket, and with Moses walking ten paces behind him carrying a fifty-eight caliber flintlock, he approached the front of the house.

As he came up the steps of the porch the Army officer greeted him with an outstretched hand. "Captain Oldham, Quartermaster, U. S. Cavalry."

"Phenias Hurtz," was the reply.

"Sir, we are here to discuss buying some horses, but we can't do business with anyone who has a slave." He pointed to Moses who was just starting up the steps of the porch.

"Ya'all came to the right place then," said Moses, without being spoken to, as he ambled up the steps and dropped into a rocking chair on the porch.

"Yes," said Phenias. "This is my friend Moses. I'll bet he'd be delighted to show you some of the finest horses in the west."

"Yes, Sa," said Moses with a big grin. "I could show ya'all some real fine horses, and we has some real fast Indian ponies, too."

"Mr. Hurtz," the captain said, turning to face the passing detachment on the road a hundred feet away. He set his gaze on the passing troops as if unsure as to which man he was talking. "I need to purchase two four-ups of wagon horses for pulling our caissons and three riding horses to replace some that have been lost to night time thievery by the savages."

"We would be happy to get you those horses, Captain, but you have to be prepared to pay for them," said Phenias.

"Lieutenant," the senior officer said, "Pay this man for eleven horses."

The younger officer opened a small book, looked up a couple of prices, figured and made notes in his book and then opened a pouch and handed Mr. Hurtz several gold and silver coins.

Phenias looked at the money and then at Captain Oldham. "I think you have overpaid for those horses, Sir."

"What you have been paid is the going rate for horses purchased by the U.S. Army," said Captain Oldham, descending the steps. "Now, let's go get those horses."

Within an hour, and with the help of mounted men from the

troop, the horses were rounded up and out the gate.

Moses stood next to Mr. Hurtz on the porch as he handed Captain Oldham his receipt. Mattea came out of the house to watch the departure of the horses.

"For that kind of money, I'd be tempted to deliver horses to the Army in the east," said Phenias.

"I'll tell you what, Mr. Hurtz," said Captain Oldham, "we'll be needing another twenty head of horses next month. We're setting up a new post at the foot of the Brookings Range in the Dakotah Territory. Do you know where that is?"

Phenias looked at the captain uneasily. "I know exactly where that is, but that's Sioux territory and they sure won't like seeing blue coats in their country."

"Think of it this way, you're here. This is their country, and they haven't bothered you. We're just going out to keep the road to the west and the gold mining fields open. You know, keep the peace, not make trouble for the Indians."

Captain Oldham stepped down to the first step of the porch and turned back to face Phenias. "Oh yes, I couldn't help but notice that big roan with blonde mane and tail. Bring that one along as an extra, and we'll give you double what you get for the other horses."

"You've got a deal, Sir," said Phenias as the captain and his aid mounted. They rode out the gate.

Mattea, who had been sitting in a rocker on the porch arose and came to Phenias' side as the soldiers rode away.

"Husband," she said softly, taking hold of his shirt sleeve. "He's talking about Jersey. Jersey is my horse. You said yourself, there's not another horse like her in this part of the country. I wouldn't like to see my horse sold at any price."

"Dearest," he said patiently, turning to his wife, "there is a war on in the east and the Army will be buying any horse they can. When they can't buy them, they'll confiscate them in the name of the government. With the money we get from the sale of those horses, we can double our herd."

Mattea felt frustrated and angry even through she understood the business part of it. There was wisdom in selling Jersey, but she loved that horse. She had worked and trained that horse. It was her horse.

The month passed, and in the first days of June, Mr. Hurtz and Joshua packed up their mules, tied a string of ten horses and one of eleven and headed out the gate for the Dakotah Territory.

Mattea stood on the porch and watched. Tears danced in her eyes as she saw her beautiful horse, Jersey, go out of sight. Jersey had been her wedding present from Mr. Hurtz four years before. As far as she was concerned, Jersey was being sold so some soldier could sit atop the most beautiful horse in this part of the country.

"Well," said Moses, coming up the step, "maybe we can finish that batch of cheese we've been working on and maybe make some more butter."

Butter and cheese had become Mattea's stock in trade in the Sheteck Lake settlement. She traded for materials and all kinds of goods at the general store. She also traded with travelers that passed along the road. New Ulm was nearly seventy miles away, but there were travelers on the road every few days.

During the third week of June, Mr. Johnson, the Post Rider, came up in a hurry and rode into the yard. Moses saw him coming through the gate, his horse at a dead run, and ran out to see what the big rush was about.

"Indians!" Johnson exclaimed. "Those savages were counting coup on my head. They broke from the brush screaming and yelling. There were four of them. They were wearing war paint! They overtook me. I thought I was dead for sure, but they just rode up and tapped me on the shoulders and head with their lances."

Mattea quickly ushered Mr. Johnson into the house and sat him down to a cold roast pork sandwich and a glass of milk. Eating seemed to calm his nerves somewhat. Although less agitated, he kept recounting the story. Each time, he remembered more details of the incident: the horses, the faces, the screams, the chants and the lances.

After eating, Mr. Johnson was calm. Moses asked Mr. Johnson out on the porch to join him for a smoke. Mr. Johnson lit his pipe and passed the match to Moses.

After a long draw on his pipe, Mr. Johnson said, "There is just no way for a post rider to protect himself, Moses. Our horses are big and strong to last the trek of three days, but we're not allowed to carry guns for our protection because of the weight. We just have to do our best. That just isn't good enough when you run into savages on the road."

Moses eyed the smallish man for a moment. "You know," he said, smiling. "I bet we can fix your problem. Come with me to the barn."

The barn was large with the tack and harness room set in the center of the east wall.

"Come in here. We have the answer," said Moses with a grin.

On the far side of the room sat a lady's lightweight riding saddle, no pommel, but plenty of padding.

"That little saddle will never fit on my big old horse," scoffed Mr. Johnson.

"You won't ride your horse, you'll ride this one," said Moses, pointing to a black Indian pony in a shoeing stall. The pony was thinner and leaner than Johnson's horse, but sturdy and well muscled.

Moses opened a large cabinet and withdrew a six-shot revolver with a holster designed to fit over a man's shoulder and mount the firearm on his chest. "You can take off your boots and put this on," he said as he handed the gun to Mr. Johnson.

"Take off my boots?" Mr. Johnson growled. "Exactly, what do you mean?"

"Those big old, thick soled boots you wear, are heavy. You can wear lighter shoes, moccasins or no shoes at all and that will make you lighter. You dress this way and your little Indian pony will outrun any war party you come across."

"Okay, I understand what you are telling me, but how do I tie on my mail pouch?" Mr. Johnson asked.

"You wear it on your back like one of those infantry soldiers

91

you see marching by now and then," answered Moses.

Within the hour, Mr. Johnson galloped out of the gate on his new pony. He rode with no shoes. Saying he would get new moccasins at Mr. Esleck's store when he got into Sheteck Lake.

The next day, Mr. Johnson stopped by the Hurtz place to express his appreciation to Moses for the new horse. "I feel like I can outrun the wind on this pony," he said. "I can travel easier and faster than I ever have before."

In the weeks that followed, Mr. Johnson stopped by regularly, bringing the mail and telling tales of seeing small bands of Indians along the road. None came close as he could easily outdistance any braves that pursued him.

The days of summer passed slowly. Moses and Mattea spent their days doing their domestic chores around the place. They churned butter and made cheese, tended the livestock and the growing crops.

Mattea began to watch the road for the return of her husband, but he did not come. When he planned his trip to Dakotah, he said that he would be home by mid July. Every day she was disappointed. She began to feel concerned about his absence.

One morning in late July, Moses came rushing into the house. "We have a problem," he said, a concerned look on his face. "During the night, the Sioux slipped onto the place and stole all but three of our horses."

"Did you look for sign that it was Sioux?" Mattea. asked

"I am sure it was Sioux. There were tracks of six or eight different ponies. I'm going to ride into Sheteck Lake and see if there has been any other raids in the area."

While Moses was gone, Mattea busied herself with normal chores and continued looking often at the road for the happy sight of her husband's return.

In a few hours, Moses was back with news. "There were several other raids on outlying farms last night. Lots of horses have disappeared in the last couple of days. A twenty-two wagon train about thirty miles down the road to the west had most of their stock stolen from their grazing area by a night raid." Moses tugged nervously at his left ear. "Do you think we should pack up and move into Sheteck Lake?"

"No." said Mattea, firmly. "This is our home. If the Indians want us to leave, they will have to tell us to leave. Phenias will be home any day and I wouldn't want him to come home to an empty house."

In the days that followed, Mattea paid close attention to the whereabouts of her children, never allowing Phillip to wander far from the house while playing.

On the afternoon of the 19th of August, Mr. Johnson, the post rider, stopped on his way into Sheteck Lake. He was driving a small two seat carriage. He left his sulky and came up on the porch where Mattea sat mending one of Phillip's shirts.

"Here's your letter, Ma'am," he said as he dropped into a rocking chair. "What do you make of all this Indian trouble?"

"What Indian trouble?" asked Mattea.

"One thing for sure," he replied as he dug out his pipe and lit it. "Something's wrong. Other than the two or three run-ins I've had on the road, I haven't seen an Indian all summer. Usually, you see them everywhere. Have you seen any? I know you trade them for chickens and beef and vegetables."

"You're right," said Mattea, feeling a little uneasy. "I usually see several and trade with at least a dozen during a normal summer, but this year, we haven't seen any."

"That's the problem," continued Mr. Johnson, gesturing with his pipe. "They must be up to something. Their absence is very suspicious. What about this horse stealing? I hear that they have stolen enough horses to mount a whole regiment of cavalry."

Moses emerged from the barn and came to join the conversation which had turned to the hot dry weather, the need for rain, and the slow ripening of the corn.

After a few minutes, Mr. Johnson tapped his pipe on the sole of his left moccasin, dumping the ash into his hand. "I best be going. I've got lots of mail for Sheteck Lake this trip. There must be sixty permanent residents there now."

He stepped into his sulky and drove out through the gate, back onto the road and turned south at the junction toward Sheteck Lake.

***

It was five o'clock in the morning of August 20th, the beginning of a bright warm day. Another dry day in southwestern Minnesota.

Mattea took her two pails, went to the barn and began milking as she did every day.

She was startled by an unfamiliar sound. She heard the drum beat of many horses hooves crossing the road and coming into the yard. Mattea's stomach tightened, and her heart quickened. It was not the hollow clopping of shod horses, but the soft pounding of unshod hooves.

Mattea dashed through the side door of the barn to the house as twenty Sioux braves covered in war paint reined to a stop and dismounted in front of her house. Seven came into the house. Five that she knew sat down at the table and began smoking small pipes as was their custom when entering the lodge of friends or family.

Mattea repressed her anguish and shock. "Cinder Horse, why have you come to my home?"

"Little Fire Hair," he responded, blowing out a large smoke ring, "we are here to give you your life. Today, this land is going to be washed clean with the blood of the whites. They will be swept away by the people."

Mattea's children, asleep in their room, awoke and Josie began to cry. Moses walked softly in from his room, picked her up and carried her out the back door and around toward the front of the house.

A brave standing inside, near the front door, pulled the door open, stepped out on the porch and fired his flintlock at Moses. The bullet hit him in the chest and he fell backward, dead. A cloud of dust flew up around his body as it struck the dry earth. Josie remained quiet in his arms. With a war whoop the brave pulled his knife and bounded off the porch. Scalping and mutilating the corpse was very important.

Cinder Horse was right behind the brave, shouting, "Bring me the child!"

A second brave jumped over the porch rail, picked up Josie gently, and handed her up to Cinder Horse.

Cinder Horse brought Josie and placed her in Mattea's arms. Another brave brought Phillip out of his bedroom in his night shirt. Phillip quickly wrapped his arms around his mother's leg for security.

As if the gun shot was some hideous prearranged signal, all of the braves outside came into the house, women and children who had been concealed, suddenly appeared, smashing, tearing, ripping and breaking furniture. Dishes and glassware were smashed. Featherbeds were sliced open and their inside scattered throughout the house and into the yard.

Some of the squaws ripped the boards off of the chicken coop and built a fire in the middle of the barnyard. Chickens were killed, cleaned and cooked on the spot.

The smoke house and cellar were opened, their contents strewn all over the yard. Pigs, running around squealing in the commotion, were shot with arrows or speared for sport. The cows broke through the fence and raced away down the south pasture.

Thirty blocks of cheese and two hundred pounds of butter were pulled from the cellar and thrown into the yard to waste along with sacks of onions, potatoes and carrots. All of Mattea's hard work was being viciously destroyed.

Mattea and her children were jerked out onto the front porch as the rampage continued inside her home. She felt numb. Awake, but not feeling. She felt fear, anger, disgust and dread, but there was nothing she could do. She held her children close to her, knowing she must protect them no matter what. There were no tears. She could not allow the Sioux to see any sign of weakness.

"You, Little Fire Hair, will be allowed to live," said Cinder Horse, looking hard into her eyes. "You must give no alarm. You must follow the old trail. The Sioux trail, three miles to the south. You can follow it to New Ulm and to your mother." He smiled. "You must not go by the Post Road for that road is being used by the people and if they see you, they *will* kill you. All other whites must die," he continued. "You must promise to give no alarm. If you do, you will be killed."

A harsh, unfamiliar look crossed his face, "I am a shaman of the people, now. All whites must go. Our land shall be washed clean of the whites by their blood."

Mattea was careful to keep Phillip from seeing Moses' body as they were forced down the stairs and out into the road. Six braves mounted and led Cinder's horse to him. The horse was *Jersey*! Mattea would not have to wait for her husband to come home. The sight of Mattea's beloved horse told her of his fate.

Cinder Horse had killed her good friend, Moses. She would not allow him to know that he had killed the man she loved. He would not have the satisfaction of knowing that Jersey was her horse. She must think of the living -- of her children.

"Please, Cinder," she implored. "Can I have clothes for my children? They are almost naked. Can I have a shawl or at least my bonnet?"

Cinder mounted his horse, raised his chin and declared, "You have your life. That is enough."

Mattea was pushed, prodded and shoved along the Sheteck Post Road for three miles to the south. Phillip was frightened and virtually bounced along beside her, holding tight to her hand. A long grass-covered prairie valley extended in front of her to the east.

"This is a trail used by the people since the time of my father's father. Follow this trail and go to your mother," said Cinder Horse. "Remember," he commanded in a stern voice, "do not go near the lodges at Sheteck Lake! Do not go near the Post Road and do not give an alarm or you and your children will die." He prodded her with the tip of his war lance. "Go to your mother!"

She looked at the war lance that was held in front of her face. There was blood on the spear head and on the shaft. She recoiled when she recognized the blond hair of her neighbor,

Molly Ferguson, hanging alongside three others on the shaft. *That dark hair! Could that be all that is left of my beloved husband?* she thought.

Mattea turned and started to walk, carrying Josie close to her breast. Her anger could not be controlled any longer. She spun around and spoke back to the Indian. "This is not the moon for taking a name, but I take back the name I gave to you. You will no longer be known as Cinder Horse. From this day forward, you will be known to all the people and white men alike, as Crazy Horse!"

The brave flinched, appearing shocked and hurt. He jammed his war lance down into the ground and screamed in a voice of disgust, "Go to your mother!"

The Indians wheeled their horses, and Mattea was alone on the prairie with her half-naked children, without food, water or shade from the heat of the blazing summer sun.

The sky was clear, and the sun shone brighter than usual. The morning dew lay heavy on the grass, and it was cold on Phillip's bare feet. He pressed close to his mother for warmth.

"Mommy," he pleaded, "I don't like it here. Let's go home." He began to cry pitifully. He was not interested in continuing the cheerless walk.

As she turned away from her home, Mattea's emotions were raging. Fear for her children and herself, confusion as to the whereabouts of her husband, but most of all, anger filled her soul.

Carrying Josie in her left arm, she swept Phillip up in her right arm, and ran toward the east. Rage burning hot in her breast.

"I've always been good to the Sioux!" she said aloud, as she climbed the rise at the end of the valley and came out onto the open prairie. "My family has always lived in peace and so have all the people of the settlement."

She changed her direction, a little to the right as she could hear an occasional war whoop carried on the breeze from her home. Smoke was pluming upward from the cooking fire in the barnyard, but there was no smoke from her house nor her barn. The Indians had apparently chosen not to burn the house, a large fire could be seen for many miles. Her father had taught her that on the flat prairie, you can stand in any one place and the horizon is fourteen miles away in any direction. A large fire would certainly put people on their guard. Her family farm was growing smaller on the horizon behind her.

"How could Cinder Horse, *Crazy Horse from now on*, allow this to happen? I am responsible for saving his life! He wouldn't even be alive if it wasn't for me," she said aloud as she walked on.

She began to slow her pace as she realized that she was still alive, *because of him*. A life for a life. That was all he could give her and no more.

Nearly stumbling, Mattea came to a halt and sat down with the children. She had run almost two miles. Slowly, she turned and looked back toward her home. It was all gone. It looked like several black postage stamps now, with a wisp of white smoke trailing upward. All she had worked for from dawn until dusk every day, was gone.

The anger that had filled her was giving way to fear. Where would they go? Where would they sleep? What would they eat? Mattea felt nearly panic stricken. She wanted to jump up and down and scream!

Phillip, who had stopped pleading for his morning beverage of milk, was already twenty yards ahead, running and jumping, trying to catch a passing grasshopper. Mattea stood up. She picked up Josie who was pulling handfuls of grass and trying to eat them. The baby gooed and laughed as Mattea lifted her. "Thank you, God," Mattea prayed aloud as she walked along behind her son. "My boy has no idea what is happening. He thinks we are just out for a jaunt." *Let him enjoy the walk while he can*, she thought to herself.

Mattea heard two gun shots from behind her and to the south. She knew that sound spelled the death of her neighbor, Mr. Cook.

With death behind her and all the horrors of starvation before her, there was no alternative but to go on. For her children, anything except death at the hands of the merciless savages; even starvation on the prairie was better.

Josie was getting fussy and tired of being carried. Mattea found a low spot with quite tall grass and settled down to rest and nurse Josie. It was an ideal spot to keep them from view and allow them to rest while she nursed the baby.

When Josie had finished nursing, Mattea placed her near the top of her shoulder and patted her gently until the baby burped. "It is nice to know," she said softly, wiping Josie's chin with her dress, "you won't starve, my little angel."

Phillip came and sat by his mother. "Mommy, I need to go home. I'm tired," he said taking hold of her dress.

"Not yet, Son," Mattea replied. Trying to be calm, she rubbed his head. "You've been a very brave big boy coming all this way with me, we still have a little farther to go."

Phillip smiled and laid down next to his mother to rest.

After a few minutes, she let the baby down to crawl, and crawl away she did, but not too far. Mattea knew there would be no carrying Josie anywhere if she didn't get to play.

Mattea was still in denial. She refused to let herself think about the terrible things that were happening to her and her loved ones, for fear she might panic. She sat and watched the baby play and giggle for a while. She breathed the freshness of the air, felt the warmth in the breeze and tried to be thankful to be alive.

She wanted to stay right there and wait for someone to come and get them, but she knew better than that. There was no one, and she knew she must go on. As she stood up, she realized that Phillip was asleep.

"Phillip." Mattea shook her son. "We must go." He did not budge. She wondered how she was going to carry both children.

She looked around, trying to think of something. Then exclaimed, "Ahah!" She pulled up her dress and began ripping out the underskirt. Moments later, she had a long piece of cloth she used as a sling to tie the baby onto her back. She picked up Phillip, still asleep and began walking again.

The clouds were rolling in and although there was a warm breeze, Mattea knew it would rain soon. It was slow going, carrying both children, but she was glad Phillip was sleeping. Josie was sighing softly. Mattea knew she, too, must sleep soon.

With the children quiet, Mattea began to think of Jersey, the horse *Crazy Horse* was riding. Her horse! She began to accept the fact that Phineas was gone. She tried to imagine some way that it was not true and at any moment, he would ride over the hill and save her, wrapping her in his strong arms.

A single rain drop on her forehead brought her back to reality. She blinked and felt as if her heart had been ripped out. There seemed to be a huge hollow spot where it had been. Her stomach seemed to fill with butterflies, and she felt very weak. Her life had been stolen! Her husband, her home, her security -- all gone! There was no one to console her.

She wished for her mother. She wanted to cry out like a little girl and have her mother say, "It's all right." *Why didn't I go east with my parents? Was I foolish to think I could make it out here in the wilds of the western frontier?* she thought.

In the middle of the afternoon, a summer thunderstorm appeared on the western horizon and slowly crept up on Mattea and the children. There was little wind, but the thunder and lightning were unusually violent. As evening approached, the thunder and lightning subsided but the rain continued to fall steadily.

At least I won't die of thirst or be burned by the sun in this downpour, she thought.

During the storm, Mattea lost the trail. The sun was obscured by the heavy cloud cover and there were no landmarks. The steady rain continued well into the night.

Water was beginning to pond on the open prairie. She could find no trees nor even brush to shelter under, so when she came upon a slight rise in the landscape she laid her children down to rest for the night. She had nothing to put over the children for their protection, so she sat beside and leaned over them to protect them from the rain and the chilling blast of the cooling night air.

"Mommy! Mommy! I'm hungry," pleaded Phillip, his tears mixed with rain on his little face.

"Just lie down and rest, Son." said Mattea as she patted his head.

Hungry, weary and wet, Phillip fell asleep and slept until morning, but Josie fretted and squirmed as the night wore away.

As soon as there was enough light to see, Mattea looked around, trying to get her bearings. She sighed a deep sigh, picked up Josie, took Phillip's hand and began to walk. There was a hollow nervous feeling in the pit of her stomach. She was too overwhelmed to feel the hunger that dogged her son. After about two hours, she sat down to nurse Josie.

She knew the trail was lost, but she was not fully conscious of it until she could hear war whoops carried on the breeze and the report of rifle fire in the distance. To her amazement, she had lost her way and was going toward, not away from, Sheteck Lake. She rose, scooping Josie close to her breast, turned and renewed her effort in the opposite direction. She pressed on with increased energy.

She could not see a trail. She could only pray that she was going in the right direction this time.

The sun was rising warm in the eastern sky, but so much water on the prairie just turned the air into mist. The warmth of the sun could not be felt for the fog that gathered around them, so heavy the sun could not be seen. The mist hung wet in the air. Their clothes did not dry the entire day.

Mattea did not feel her hunger, Josie was a nursing infant and did not suffer, but her brother was wracked with hunger pangs and pleaded constantly for food, at least a glass of his favorite beverage, milk.

Mattea's heart was breaking. She could hardly bear the crying of her child for food, but there was nothing she could do.

For most of his ordeal, Phillip had trudged along at his mother's side, always thinking of food, only occasionally getting distracted and running a short distance ahead. As evening of the second day of their ordeal approached, Phillip was running ahead. He stopped on a little rise.

"Mommy, Mommy!" he exclaimed. "I found our road. We can go home!"

In moments, Mattea was at his side. Yes, they had found the Post Road, and she recognized where she was. Her heart sank. She must have been wandering in circles. They were four miles from home. She felt exhausted and discouraged.

As night fell, she knew her journey had just begun. She took Phillip's hand and began down the road toward New Ulm. Only sixty-four miles to go. She was happy to be on this familiar road, and it came to her that it would be better to die here in this familiar place than to perish somewhere out on the great trackless prairie.

After it had become quite dark, Mattea stopped and they spent the night as they had the night before. Once gain, Mattea did not sleep.

Phillip could not settle down, turning restlessly and moaning. He began to vomit. After an hour of vomiting and dry heaves, he fell asleep exhausted, cold and damp.

When morning came, the sun broke the horizon to the east, and they started walking again. It was foggy, and the tall grass was wet. The road, being little traveled, the narrow wheel ruts had tall grass growing up in the middle, and it spread more dampness to their clothes which were not yet dry.

Phillip was so sick he could not walk, so Mattea had to carry him. Her own strength was wanning. She found she was no longer able to carry both children at once.

"Mommy," Phillip looked up at his mother, as he slumped to the ground. "I don't feel so good, Mommy."

Mattea looked at her son. His hair was almost black from moisture. He looked very pitiful with his big eyes shallow and sunken.

Mattea looked at the sky speaking directly to God. "Why?" she cried out, startling Josie. "Lord in Heaven! Why is this happening? What have I done? Why should I and my children, have to die out here with the animals?" She dropped to her knees. Her shoulders slumped forward. She prayed.

A soft breeze rustled the tall grass around her, the mist seemed to lift all at once and a warm burst of sunlight swept the spot where she and the children were huddled.

A voice seemed to come to her in her anxious heart, "Mattea. You are not going to die."

"Stay right here in the grass, Phillip. Mommy will be right back for you. We are not going to die." She placed her hand on Phillip's cheek, "Before this day is over, we will find food, my precious son."

One at a time, she carried the children up the road for a quarter of a mile, setting them down while she returned for the other. Using this method to transport her children, Mattea traveled twelve miles.

Phillip no longer asked for food, but drank frequently from the pools of rain water at the side of the road. After many hours, completely exhausted, they arrived at Dutch Charlie's place about sixteen miles from Sheteck Lake just before sunset.

All day, Mattea had sustained her hope by the expectation of relief. Her heart leaped with joy as she approached the house.

To her agonizing disappointment, she found the house to be empty. It had not been raided by the Indians. Not one piece of food or clothing remained. She slumped down on the floor, exhaustion and despair wracking her body and spirit. She fell into unconsciousness.

The cries of her children aroused her, and she began to look for food.

Mattea had promised Phillip food when they reached Dutch Charlie's. When none was found, he began to cry bitterly.

Mattea found some green corn and tried to eat it, but her stomach would not tolerate it and it came right back up. In the garden, she also found carrots and onions which she ate raw, because she did not have a fire.

Phillip began to vomit again. She offered him a piece of carrot, but he could not eat it. It was too dark to continue the search for food, so they retired to a nearby cornfield and slept, much as they had the previous two nights. This night however, Mattea slept.

At daybreak, Mattea sat up and touched her son's cheek. "Phillip, you be a brave boy and stay here in the cornfield with sister for me. I'm going to find you something to eat."

Returning to the farmhouse, she went instinctively to the smoke house. She stirred through the ashes of the burn pile next to the smokehouse and found a discarded ham bone. To her delight, there was about a pound of meat on the bone that had not burned nor decayed. The small amount of meat was clean, rich and well cured.

"Phillip, Phillip!" she exclaimed as she rushed through the cornfield to where her babies waited. "Look, Son. Mommy has some food for you."

Mattea fed Phillip little bits of ham, causing his vomiting to stop and he started feeling better.

Mattea spent an hour gathering carrots and onions from the garden and removing the last of the ham from the bone. She used the torn off section of her dress and fashioned a rucksack in which to carry the food.

It would be twenty-five miles to their next objective, the home of Mr. Brown.

This day went much as the day before. Phillip was getting stronger and could again walk, but he would tire out and just lie down on the road. Mattea continued to walk ahead a quarter of a mile, lay a child in the grass and return for the other child. This went on for most of the day. When night came, the family slipped off the road to a spot on the other side of a rise and fell asleep.

The morning of the fifth day of their perilous trek found Phillip much stronger and nearly recovered from his hunger. He was able to walk all day on his own.

The day passed more easily, and the family walked with less anguish and torment.

About three miles from the home of Mr. Brown Phillip looked back at the western horizon and stopped walking. Sensing he was falling behind, Mattea turned to call for him. "Phil..." her eyes caught the skyline. There were men and horses on the skyline coming down the road behind her from the west. She rushed back to Phillip, took his hand and resumed walking resolutely.

"Well, my son," she spoke softly to Phillip, "if we are to die at the hands of savages after all we have been through, then this means the Lord has spared us for this purpose."

She continued to walk, listening for the approach of her pursuers. Soon, she could hear the steady *"clop, clop, clop"* of a shod horse walking slowly.

Probably a horse stolen from the settlement, she thought. She wanted to grab the children and run, but she had no strength left.

"Mattea. Mattea Hurtz." A familiar voice came from behind her.

Mattea turned to see Mr. Johnson, the post rider, leading a horse pulling a sulky. In the sulky, rode two of her good neighbors from the Sheteck Lake settlement.

Mattea was so relieved that it was not Indians, but people she knew, that her legs wobbled out from under her. She fell to her knees weeping aloud.

Phillip patted her shoulder and spoke in a soft voice, "Don't cry, Mommy. It's just Mr. Johnson and Mr. Ireland."

The sulky came alongside Mattea and the children and stopped. Each member of the tiny group related their story to Mattea.

Mr. Ireland, had been hit by eight balls and was still able to walk, and had done so for much of the way. Mrs. Esleck, the other person, could not walk, having been shot in the foot, once in the side and once in the arm.

Mrs. Esleck's husband had been killed outright and her ten-year-old son wounded so badly he had to be left at the settlement.

Mrs. Esleck and Mr. Ireland had struggled up the post road until overtaken by Mr. Johnson who had been driving a sulky that day to carry the extra mail. There had been a large quantity of newspapers telling the stories of the war raging between the Union and the Confederacy.

Mr. Johnson handed Josie up to Mrs. Esleck to hold while

Phillip stood between the passengers. Mattea took hold of the horse's harness for support as they continued their trek.

The small group reached Mr. Brown's house a little before sunset. A whitewashed wooden structure standing on a hillside. A small creek ran on the south side near the barn. Tall black walnut trees grew up next to the creek, creating a lovely setting for the Brown farm. Except for the fact that there was no livestock about, there was a feeling the family was home, perhaps out in the fields and would be in at any moment.

Mr. Johnson reached the porch first and forced the locked door open. "I don't reckon these folks will mind us dropping in on them."

As everyone went inside, he continued, "Mattea, would you look through the pantry and see what you can find to eat? I'll go check on the smoke house and barn to make sure no one is home."

Mattea found potatoes, green corn and salt pork and began making a hearty evening meal. She also began brewing a pot of coffee. Mattea felt great! It was almost like coming home to her own kitchen.

It didn't take Mr. Johnson long to survey the barnyard. He was back in less than half an hour. "Looks like the Indians have been through here for sure. The fences are all busted down and there are three hogs and two piglets in the barnyard with about forty arrows in them."

Mattea heated water for cleaning Mr. Ireland's and Mrs. Esleck's wounds. She tore up bed sheets for bandages.

By nine o'clock everyone was as comfortable as possible. Mattea's prayers had been answered and the adequate food tasted like a banquet. Phillip and Josie were sleeping peacefully in a bed belonging to one of Mr. Brown's children. Mr. Ireland was asleep in the bed of another child and Mrs. Esleck was asleep in the Brown's bed.

Mr. Johnson and Mattea sat at the kitchen table sipping coffee. A slight breeze moved the curtains of the partially open window. Crickets filled the quiet night air with their song.

Suddenly, the crickets stopped their chorus. Mr. Johnson,

raised his left hand to tell Mattea to remain quiet. He cupped the top of the lamp on the table with his right hand and blew it out. Mr. Johnson's horse in the barnyard whinnied. Mr. Johnson pulled his pistol from its holster as he moved toward the front door.

"Oh, dear Lord," Mattea prayed quietly. "My children have come too far to be killed in their sleep. Give us your protection, Lord."

There was a soft knock at the door. "Hello, in the house. Anyone in there?" A man's voice came from the other side of the door.

Mr. Johnson pressed against the door jamb. "Who is it?"

"James Whittington, US Army."

"How many are you?"

"Just one," answered the voice from the darkness at the front of the house.

Mr. Johnson quickly unbolted the door and opened it a crack to peer out and then all the way to allow the man to enter.

"What are you doing out here by yourself?" asked Mr. Johnson as Mattea lit the lamp and cranked up the light.

"I'm not alone," said Mr. Whittington, holding up a lever action rifle and pulling off a belt of cartridge style ammunition slung across his back. "I've got Mr. Henry here with me." He patted the stock of his rifle as he handed it to Mr. Johnson for inspection. "This sweet little rifle makes me worth ten men in a fight, and I think those are pretty good odds."

"I've heard of these for years," said Mr. Johnson, "but, I've only seen one other one."

"Well, you'll be seeing a lot more as time goes on," said Whittington, removing his pistol belt and sitting down at the kitchen table.

Mattea poured a hot cup of coffee and placed it before Mr. Whittington.

"Thank you, Ma'am," he said, turning back to Mr. Johnson. "Mr. Henry put this repeating rifle together back in '60 for Winchester Arms, and they've been selling like hot cakes to men in the infantry. They're not government issue because they don't have the range or knockdown power of the Infield Rifle. The nice thing about this gun is the fact that it shoots the same .45 ammunition I use for my Colt revolver."

"You see any Indians on you way here? Where are you coming from?" asked Mr. Johnson. "Where are you going?"

Mattea placed a bowl of fried potatoes, onions and carrots in front of the new arrival.

"Hold on, just a minute," said Whittington, taking a sip of his coffee and brushing his long hair out of his eyes. "Let me eat a bite or two and I'll tell you my story. In the meantime, why don't you tell me yours?"

While Mr. Whittington finished his meal, Mattea and Mr. Johnson related their stories to him.

"Unfortunately," Whittington grimaced. "you won't have to expect the Brown family to return. I buried a family beside the road about a half day back from here. It was the Browns. A man, a woman and three children. They never had a chance. I'm sure it was the Browns as the woman was clutching a family bible and that was the name inside the cover.

"I work for the government, I hold the rank of Colonel in the Army, but as you see, I don't wear the uniform. I'm a surveyor and planner. The war is emptying our country's treasury and we need the gold and silver that is being mined in the Dakotah Territory. My job is to review the roads and conditions and plan for the fastest, most effective way to get that gold back to our government."

He pushed back from the table a little and pulled a pipe and tobacco pouch from a pocket on his shirt. "Do you mind, Ma'am?" he asked, looking at Mattea.

"No, go right ahead," she said, smiling as she cleared away the dishes.

"I was in New Ulm last week. It was raided by over two-thousand Sioux," Whittington continued as he stuck a match to his pipe. "There were almost two hundred houses burned and nearly five hundred people killed. For the most part, people were still in their night clothes. The battle lasted nearly four hours, but the settlement got organized and drove them off."

Whittington took his pipe from his mouth, blew out a puff of smoke, and a thoughtful look came over his face. "Either the folks at the settlement got organized and beat them off, or the killing wasn't so easy anymore. Folks were putting up a fight, and Indians were dying.

"These Sioux," he continued, "don't seem to engage in battle unless they have figured out exactly how it will come out."

Mr. Whittington turned to Mr. Johnson as he finished his meal. "Would you mind accompanying me? I have to put up my horse and pack mule for the night."

Mr. Johnson lit a lamp with a bail on it and went to the barn with Mr. Whittington to help him unsaddle his horse and mule.

The next morning, Mattea found clothing for herself that had been Mrs. Brown's and dressed Phillip in clothes that had belonged to little Thomas Brown. Thomas had been a year older than Phillip, but not bigger.

Mr. Johnson, accompanied by Mr. Ireland, as bad off as he was, hooked up Mr. Johnson's sulky and proceeded on the road toward New Ulm. Mattea and Mr. Whittington stood in the yard watching as the sulky pulled onto the road and continued east across the prairie. As they turned to enter the house Mr. Whittington spoke, "If you don't mind, Mattea, I am going to stay here for a couple of days with you folks. It will give my animals time to rest up, and I can study my charts."

"I'm sure we're all delighted to have you stay with us, Mr. Whittington," she replied.

"I had planned to spend the next couple of days here, whether there was anyone here or not," said Whittington as he stepped up on the porch and opened the door for her.

"Well, you certainly are welcome," said Mattea.

"I talked to Mr. Johnson and he asked me not to tell you, but I feel I should. As I came out of New Ulm," said Whittington, " I noticed the main body of the Sioux broke off and went across the prairie in a west southwest line directly toward Sheteck Lake. About twenty stayed on the road ahead of me and another dozen or so went north by northwest. I guess there must be a farm or two in that direction. They must be planning to clear the entire area of whites. The way I figure it," Whittington said, pulling the heavy door closed. "The twenty ahead of me were the ones that killed the Browns and paid a visit to your place. That means there are still a dozen or so Sioux to the north of us that could come through here at any time."

Mattea's eyes narrowed. "If they come by here, they'll have a fight on their hands."

Mattea turned her attention to Mrs. Esleck's wounds, gave her some breakfast and made sure she was comfortable. When she was done, she left Mr. Whittington studying his charts at the kitchen table and took Phillip out to explore the barnyard and garden. Avoiding the sight of the pigpen, they walked around the barn and into the chicken coop. All of the chickens had been a quick lunch for the marauding band of Indians. There were gaping holes in the back of the coop where the boards had been torn out to be used as fire wood.

"Look Mommy, eggs!" Phillip yelled, running to a nest with two eggs in it. Mattea quickly bent down and picked up the eggs and began checking all of the nests for more. When she finished, she had found fourteen eggs.

"I guess Indians don't like eggs. We know they roasted and ate all the chickens," she told Phillip as they exited the coop.

There was a rustling in the corn at the edge of the field, not twenty feet from where they were. Mattea saw the tops of several stocks of corn lean slightly and then come upright again. She grasped the corner of Phillip's sleeve and pulled him back into the chicken coop with her free hand and put her finger to her lips indicating "quiet." She stood against the wall, peering out through a crack between the boards. Her heart raced as she struggled for a better view thinking she was imagining the movement. Then it moved again. They waited and watched for several minutes. She could hear short grunting noises and then she saw it. It was one of the piglets. It had escaped the Indians and was rooting around in the cornfield.

Mattea grabbed Phillip's arm and started for the house. The eggs, nestled in the makeshift basket at the front of her dress, clicked together as they walked.

As she passed the barn, Mr. Whittington called out to her. "Where you going so fast, Ma'am?"

Mattea turned to see a friendly face. "I found some eggs in the hen house, and I thought I would make us some nice scrambled eggs and potatoes for our midday meal. What are you doing?"

Mr. Whittington joined Mattea and Phillip and accompanied them to the house. He carried his rifle with his ammunition belt slung over his shoulder. His pistol was in a holster on an ammunition belt about his waist. Mr. Whittington was taller than the average man, Mattea guessed he was well over six-feet tall. "I know you are a scout and surveyor for the government, but what about your family? Where do you come from?"

"I'm originally from Illinois. I was studying mining and working for a small arms maker in Massachusetts when the war broke out. I went to enlist in the cavalry, because I hate walking. Some government official at the school of mines decided that because I had accompanied my father on many trips west as a youngster, and understood mining, I should do the job I have."

When they reached the house, Mattea busied herself, stoking up the fire and adding wood to the kitchen stove.

Mr. Whittington watched her for a moment, then turned and opened the back door. "I think I'll bring in some more kindling for that stove," he said as he pulled the door open wide. Stopping suddenly, he removed his pistol from its holster. "You know how to use one of these?"

"Yes, I do," she said as a grin crossed her sunbaked face. "And quite well, I might say."

Mr. Whittington left his revolver on the kitchen table and closed the door behind him. Mattea watched out the kitchen window as he found the wood storage area and a sharp axe next to the barn and set to work, chopping a large arm load of kindling. When the chopping was done, he gathered up as much as he could carry and started for the house.

As he crossed the yard toward the house, his eyes scanned

the area. He stopped suddenly, his eyes straining to make out movement on the northern horizon. He looked at the chimney above the kitchen. There was a thin wisp of gray smoke rising above the house in the warm afternoon sun.

Mr. Whittington walked into the kitchen and dropped his arm load of kindling into the wood bin. "I don't want to upset you Ma'am, but there are Indians approaching from the north," he said as he picked up his revolver and placed it in his holster. "There are eight or ten riders, moving as though they are in no particular hurry. The smoke from this stove can be seen for miles!"

The shutters on the house were made of heavy two-inch boards that closed from the inside, and the front and back doors were thick with a heavy bar.

"Make sure all the shutters are closed and I'll lock and bar the front door," said Mr. Whittington as he left the kitchen.

Mattea rushed through the house making sure all the shutters were closed and barred. She ran upstairs and found Phillip and Josie. She took them into the room where Mrs. Esleck was sleeping and told them to play on the floor.

As she looked out the north facing window of Mrs. Esleck's room, she realized that all of the windows were closed. To shoot out of the gun ports in the shutters the top window sash had to be slid down. She quickly went around the upper floor opening the shutters and pushing the top window sash down and re-latching the shutter.

She felt the house was ready for the fight that would surely come. She left the children with Mrs. Esleck, who was now awake and headed down stairs. Mr. Whittington met her at the bottom of the stairs.

"Here is my revolver and a box of ammunition," he said, handing them to her. "You come and let me out the back door. I will make a stand from the barn. If I stay in here with you, they can just ride around to the barn and take my horse and mule and all of my supplies."

With her heart filled with apprehension, she closed the door and dropped the heavy bolt into place, picked up the revolver and went upstairs. She looked out the gun port at the approaching Indians. They could see the smoke easily and were starting to trot their horses toward the house. Mattea counted nine braves leading strings of horses, ten or twelve in all. They stopped about two hundred yards from the house and got off their ponies to hobble the lead horse on each string they were leading.

Mattea picked Josie off the floor and sat her on the bed next to Mrs. Esleck. She took Phillip over close to the bed so Mrs. Esleck could hold his hand.

"Phillip," she knelt, smiled and spoke softly to her boy. "Mommy is going to be shooting this gun in the house. It will make smoke and a lot of noise, so you put your fingers in your ears. I want you to be a big boy for me and hold Mrs. Esleck's hand. Can you do that for Mommy?"

Phillip grinned. "Yes, Mommy. I'll help Mrs. Esleck."

The Indians were mounted and riding at a gallop toward the front of the house. As they crossed the post road and started into the yard, a rifle shot rang out and the brave leading the band slumped from his horse and sprawled across the ground.

One brave was eyeing the upper story of the house as an entry point and stood on the back of his pony and sprang onto the roof of the front porch. The Colt .45 in Mattea's hand spoke death and the brave spun around and fell from the porch.

Another brave was running across the top of the porch roof. Mattea fired, hitting him in the leg. He rolled and bounced to the ground and pulled himself away.

Three braves ran along the side of the house, stopping at the rain barrel for cover from the barn.

Mattea rushed to the side window and without aiming, pointed the pistol through the hole and fired toward the ground. The bullet hit the side of the rain barrel and two braves leaped back as the water squirted from the barrel. The crack of Mr. Whittington's rifle rang out twice and both braves went down in a heap.

The Henry spoke again and a brave that had approached

the back door from the other side of the house went down.

There was the sound of shattering glass. Indians on the porch roof were trying to break in through the shutters. Without thinking, Mattea fired across the room at the shutter porthole. There was a scream, followed by the thump of a body dropping onto the porch roof. The banging of tomahawks on the shutter stopped momentarily. A flintlock rifle muzzle poked through the gun port from outside. Mattea dropped to a kneeling position on the floor, squeezing off a shot as she dropped. The rifle barrel jerked, pointing toward the ceiling and fired, belching a hot string of fire. The explosion was tremendous, even though there was little damage. Smoke filled the entire room and hurt Mattea's throat when she breathed.

There was a sudden crash and the room filled with the light of the afternoon sun. There, in the window, stood a familiar Indian. Mattea recognized Spotted Buffalo. He was the one who came to Mattea's father's lean-to to get the boy that had fallen into the swollen creek a dozen years before.

The warrior cocked his arm in the throwing position, his tomahawk at the ready. Mattea fired. Spotted Buffalo staggered backward and then regained his feet. His left hand had gone to his side. He pulled it away as the blood rushed forth. He grasped the window frame with his left hand and stuck his right leg through the window onto the floor. He was inside!

Out of bullets, Mattea raised the pistol over her head, ready to strike the intruder. She grabbed a metal candlestick from the bed table and held it high in her left hand to fend off the blow of the tomahawk.

All expression went out of Spotted Buffalo's face. His eyes stared into space as his knees buckled and he crumpled to the floor. He was dead. This brave that had been a friend to her father in days gone by, was about to take her life. She had done what she must.

Mattea was already reloading the revolver as she heard two more shots from the front of the house. She finished reloading and jumped to the window, the hammer on the Colt cocked back.

Looking down from the window, she could see Mr. Whittington dragging an Indian's body around the side of the house. "Are you all right?" she asked.

"I'm fine. I was just counting the dead savages. There were a couple that wanted to count me," he replied, turning his head to look up at her.

The next day was spent cleaning up after the Indian attack. Mr. Whittington dug a large hole in soft earth on the west end of the barnyard and laid the Sioux to rest. In a smaller hole nearby, he buried the pigs and piglets, telling Mattea that the pigs deserved better.

The following day, Mr. Whittington packed his mule, saddled his horse and lead them out to the side yard next to the house.

Mrs. Esleck sat in a rocking chair on the porch. She was feeling much better and growing stronger as her wounds healed. "So, it's time for you to continue your journey," she said as Mattea came out of the house carrying Josie. Phillip tagged along behind.

"Yes. I have to be on my way," replied Mr. Whittington. "I'm a little behind my schedule, I think the Sioux will be out of the area. They seem to be bent on plundering and preparing for a long winter. They may be back in the spring, but I think they have moved on for now."

Mattea gave Josie to Mrs. Esleck and went down the stairs to where Mr. Whittington was about to mount his horse. She gave him a big hug and said, "Thank you for staying with us. You have been a wonderful comfort to all of us during your visit."

"Don't mention it, Ma'am," he said, stepping up onto his horse. He turned his horse and was soon out on the post road and on his way west.

The next few days at the Brown farm passed quietly and uneventfully. Mattea found the one roaming piglet in the cornfield and butchered it for fresh meat. Some of the corn was beginning to ripen and the Indian ponies were getting fat, grazing in the barnyard pasture. Mrs. Esleck was able to walk a bit with the aid of a crutch Mr. Whittington had fashioned for her. All of her wounds were healing nicely.

Mattea was at the woodpile, cutting kindling for the cook stove. It was the first wood she had cut, as Mr. Whittington had left her quite a plentiful supply. She stopped for a moment to wipe her brow and pull the few strands of hair back that had slipped from her bandana when her gaze crossed the eastern horizon.

Riders! She could see men on horseback and a wagon. *The rescuers are coming!* Her heart jumped and she tingled all over. Mr. Johnson and Mr. Ireland had made it to New Ulm and a party had returned to take them to civilization. She dropped the axe and ran to the house to tell Mrs. Esleck and put on a fresh pot of coffee.

Twelve men came to the Brown farm to give aid and retrieve Mattea, her children and Mrs. Esleck.

After the rescue party arrived, they told of the total outbreak of hostilities and how all of the outlying settlements had been raided with all the populations massacred.

When the party reached New Ulm, Mattea and her children were taken into the home of the local minister and his family. They stayed with this family for several weeks while waiting for Mattea's father to come from New York and get them.

While she and the children were waiting, she received a letter from her mother, detailing official reports in newspapers telling how six hundred and forty-four people had been massacred on the Minnesota frontier. Chief Little Crow release two hundred and thirty-nine women and children he held hostage.

Post Script:

Fourteen hundred braves believed to have taken part in the raids in southern Minnesota in the late summer, early fall of 1862, were captured by Colonel Sibley of the US Cavalry. Three hundred and three were sentenced to hang. President Lincoln commuted the death sentences and thirty-eight were hanged on December 26, 1862. The largest mass execution in United States history.

Made in the USA
Middletown, DE
16 May 2021